Stand on My Shoulders

Treasure from the Secret Places of His Heart

By

Dotty Schmitt

ACKNOWLEDGEMENTS

*T*hroughout the writing of this book, I have felt the smile of His Presence. The writing of each chapter brought back to mind the richness of His amazing grace in my life's journey. And so it is to the great Lover of my soul, the Lord Jesus, that I first humbly bow in worship and thanksgiving.

This book is also a celebration of God's faithfulness to Charles and me and our nearly 50 years of marriage. Then there is our most extraordinary and wonderful family – Laura and George, Kai, Dylan and Brooke, Dianna and Scott, Chase and Hunter, and Jenny and Shenan – all of whom have greatly enriched my life and taught me so many invaluable lessons on life and love!

Then there is a whole group of faithful and diligent support people, without whom this book would not have been published. A huge thank you to my administrative assistant, Andrea Thompson, who, in spite of her own intense physical battle, amazingly and diligently determined to see this project to completion. You are an amazing woman of God! Thank you, dear Pirkko O'Clock, for your skill and diligence in making these pages more grammatically accurate and readable. The loving support of my wonderful team, Margaret Bell, Rosemary Parisi, Carol Clements, Gloria Ward, and Jennifer Hogue has been a great encouragement.

And what can I say about our wonderful congregation called Immanuel's Church? You, our precious church family, representing more than 65 nations, have poured your love, support, and encouragement into our lives, and been a source of much prayerful undergirding and loving inspiration.

Also, I say a big thank-you to the literally thousands of friends and colleagues over these many years who have encouraged and inspired me to write down these joyful discoveries of rich treasures found in the secret places of His heart! To all of you I declare: "The best is yet to come!"

TABLE OF CONTENTS

FOREWORD BY DOTTY'S HUSBAND

I count it an honor to write these few words for Dotty's book. I have known Dotty for over sixty years, and I can honestly say that she writes what she lives and lives what she writes. These chapters contain life-changing biblical truths that are a result of her personal encounters with her very best friend, our Lord Jesus. She lives and writes with a passion for the Word of God, and a hunger for the on-going glory and Presence of God.

Both Dotty and I have experienced many significant revival moves of God and are more passionate for a fresh move of His Holy Spirit in this generation than ever before. To increasingly become people who are lovers of truth and lovers of His Presence is the heart of this book.

The secret [of the sweet, satisfying
companionship] of the Lord have they who
fear (revere and worship) Him, and He will
show them His covenant and reveal to them its
[deep, inner] meaning.
Psalm 25:14 Amplified

Dotty writes especially with the next generation in view. "Things we have heard and known . . . we will not hide . . . we will tell the next generation the praiseworthy deeds of the Lord . . . so the next generation would know them, even the children yet to be born, and they in turn would tell their children. Then they would put their trust in God and not forget his deeds but would keep his commands" (Psalm 78 NIV). God is beginning to stir afresh in a new generation – our children and our grandchildren. I pray that they shall arise as the veritable army of God in these last days to declare the nearness of the awesome Day of God and "speed its coming" (2 Peter 3:12)!

In the language of Proverbs, chapter 31, I can say of Dotty –

"A wife of noble character who can find?
She is worth far more than rubies.
Her husband has full confidence in her. . .

She speaks with wisdom,
And faithful instruction is on her tongue. . .

Her children arise and call her blessed;
Her husband also, and he praises her:
'Many women do noble things,
But you surpass them all'. . ."

- Charles P. Schmitt

IN OUR SECRET PLACE

WHERE I MEET WITH YOU
THERE'S JUST YOU AND ME
O LOVER OF MY SOUL

IN OUR SECRET PLACE
WHERE THE WORLD IS DIM
FOR THERE'S JUST YOUR FACE
O LOVER OF MY SOUL

(Chorus)
CALL MY NAME
SING TO ME
DRAW ME CLOSE
LET ME FEEL YOUR HEART
AND I'LL CALL YOUR NAME
JESUS
I WILL DRAW CLOSE
LET YOU FEEL MY HEART
IN OUR SECRET PLACE

WHERE NO FEAR CAN COME
THERE YOU KISS MY TEARS
O LOVER OF MY SOUL
GROWS STRONG
O LOVER OF MY SOUL
(Chorus)

(Ending)
IN OUR SECRET PLACE
LORD I'LL COME TO YOU
LORD I'LL RUN TO YOU
LORD YOU WAIT FOR ME
IN OUR SECRET PLACE
(2x)

Stand on My Shoulders

Treasures from the Secret Places of His Heart

A Mandate Given

O God, You have taught me from my youth;
and to this day I declare Your wondrous works.
Now also when I am old and gray headed, O
God, do not forsake me, until I declare Your
strength to this generation,
Your power to everyone who is to come.
Psalm 71:17,18

*C*harles and I were watching the national news when the tragedy of the Columbine High School Massacre in Littleton, Colorado, came on the screen. It was Tuesday, April 20, 1999. As we watched in shock and horror the killing of 12 students and a teacher, a familiar face appeared on the screen. It was Darrell Scott, the father of one of the murdered students, Rachel Joy.*

We both sat up virtually speechless. We had known Darrell and Beth since the 70s. We were stunned as we watched the awful events of that horrendous day swirling around this family we knew. How could two teenagers become so lost and deceived that they would commit such an act of violence or even conceive it?

Through a series of unfolding events, including the Scotts' meeting with President and Mrs. Clinton in the White House, Darrell and his son Craig came to Washington, D.C. We invited them to share their tragic but powerful testimony with young people from our area. I will never forget that night. Hundreds of youth filled our sanctuary.

As Craig shared the heart-rending account of lying on the library floor between two of his good friends, the young people in the sanctuary sat in stunned silence. As Craig lay there, the shooters went into the hall. He prayed that the Lord would take away his fear and give him courage. He believed the Lord spoke clearly to him that he was to get up, get out, and take everyone with him. When the shooters reentered the library to finish the job of killing, they found it empty. Because of Craig's courage, all remaining students in the library had been led to safety, including one who had been shot in the shoulder.

As I was listening, I became very aware of the fact that I was holding in my arms my six-week-old grandson. My heart was crying out, "Lord, what kind of a world has Chase been born into?" Slowly a peace encompassed me, and I heard: "A world in which I am still sovereign and in control. A world in which I AM; and will pour out my Spirit on all people, especially on the youth."

> *And it shall come to pass afterward that I will*
> *pour out My Spirit on all flesh; your sons and*
> *your daughters shall prophesy, your old men*
> *shall dream dreams, your young men shall see*
> *visions. And also on My menservants and on*

My maidservants I will pour out My Spirit in those days.
Joel 2:28,29

As I sat there, in the midst of hundreds of teens, I felt an urgency to make a difference in their world. I wanted to hold each of them and pour into them the years of learning of His heart and of His ways. A prayer and cry erupted from deep within my heart: "Lord, capture their hearts, ruin them for Yourself, open Your Word to them, and give them a deep hunger for the secret place of rich communion with Yourself."

As Darrell finished his powerful and riveting sharing, he concluded by saying: "Yes, you must be willing to die for Jesus, but tonight I am asking you: are you willing to radically live for Jesus?" The sanctuary was pregnant with His Presence. Darrell stepped back, and quietly waited. No one moved. As I looked around, I knew that numbers of these young people were living a compromised lifestyle. I could feel the battle within them taking place.

His Presence brooded over us, and still no one moved. After what felt like a long time, small groups of youth came forward to kneel in surrender to the Lord. Soon the whole front, as well as the platform was filled with youth calling out to the Lord. Still holding six-week-old Chase in my arms, I walked up to the large cross in the front of the platform and held him up to the Lord. With tears streaming down my face I cried out: "Lord, mark him for your kingdom. May he love and serve you all the days of his life."

As I stood there in the midst of hundreds of young people, I heard His voice: "Are you willing for this next generation to stand on your shoulders and go farther than you have gone?" "Yes, Lord, show my generation how to pour and impart into those who will follow us in the furthering of your kingdom and in preparing the way for Your return."

So, my precious reader, you are holding this book in your hands! It is my story of having found rich, precious treasure in my beloved Lord. This treasure was unearthed in the everyday practicalities of living life. It is the prayer of my heart that regardless of your age, you will tell your story to every and all generations. Each of us has a powerful and unique story to tell of Jesus' love, grace, and mercy. We each have a story to tell to our families, friends, and to future generations. Our Lord is always wooing us to the deeper places of communion and intimacy with Himself. Once you have experienced the beauty of the secret place, you will hunger for more of the Spirit and for more of the revelation of His Word. Once you have encountered the glory of His Presence, your face will also shine with the oil of His Spirit, and you will become a carrier and imparter of His glory to every generation of people you encounter.

So whether you are a father or mother in the faith, or a son or daughter who is just beginning the journey, I invite you to join me in the story of my own treasure hunt into the secret places of His heart. And let's remember and ponder together Paul's words concerning Jesus:

. . .in whom are hidden all the treasures of
wisdom and knowledge.
Colossians 2:3

Included in the following pages are some chapters written by my own beloved daughters, Laura, Dianna, and Jenny. Each is now married and each has her own story to tell. There is no greater earthly joy than to see your children (both physical and spiritual) and grandchildren on their own "treasure hunt" in the things of the Lord.

For I rejoiced greatly when brethren came and
testified of the truth that is in you, just as you
walk in the truth. I have no greater joy than to
hear that my children walk in truth.
3 John 3,4

It is for my daughters and their husbands, George, Scott, and Shenan, as well as for our precious grandchildren, Chase, Kai, Dylan, Brook, and Hunter, that I declare this covenant promise of blessing:

"As for Me," says the LORD, "this is My
covenant with them: My Spirit who is upon you,
and My words which I have put in your mouth,
shall not depart from your mouth, nor from
the mouth of your descendants, nor from the
mouth of your descendants' descendants," says
the LORD, "from this time and forevermore."
Isaiah 59:21

Essential to the telling of my story is the influence, inspiration, and supportive Presence of my beloved husband, Charles. Before we were married, the Lord gave me this precious promise for our life together:

> *. . .then I will give them one heart and one way,*
> *that they may fear Me forever, for the good of*
> *them and their children after them.*
> Jeremiah 32:39

May you, my beloved ones and your generation, help to hasten the glorious day of the Lord! "Come, Lord Jesus, come."

Father, I speak blessing, favor, and revelation over every person who reads and reflects upon the treasure of Your Word in these following pages. May each one be further envisioned, equipped, and empowered to dig deeper into the revelation of Your Word, and to find new strength and determination to tell their own story of Your amazing grace to all around them.

* For Rachel's complete story we recommend *Rachel's Tears* by Beth and Darrell Scott, Thomas Nelson publishers.

A Captured Heart

I will run the course of Your commandments,
for You shall enlarge my heart.
Psalm 119:32

Will I ever forget the anticipation that filled my heart on that early evening in March, 1951! I had been invited to a youth group that was actually meeting in my own church basement. From the age of 5, I had been sent with a teenage girl from my apartment complex to the neighborhood church of Trinity Reformed. I enjoyed accumulating all the Sunday school buttons, but didn't really understand all this stuff about God. But it was fun being with friends from the neighborhood.

As I walked the three blocks to the church building, little did I know that I was on my way to a divine appointment. All I was thinking about was that I'd be with some friends, and I believe all the Lord was thinking about was that He was waiting to have a meeting with a twelve-year-old, insecure, and often ill girl, and that He would forever change her and the course of her life. As with all of us, He waits, He longs, and He seeks until He finds us!

*"For thus says the Lord God: 'Indeed I Myself
will search for My sheep and seek them out. As
a shepherd seeks out his flock on the day he is
among his scattered sheep. . . .'"*
Ezekiel 34:11,12a

*". . .for the Son of Man has come to seek and to
save that which was lost."*
Luke 19:10

*"But the hour is coming, and now is, when the
true worshipers will worship the Father in spirit
and truth; for the Father is seeking such to
worship Him."*
John 4:23

As I sat there listening to our pastor's daughters teach us from a flannel graph lesson on the death and resurrection of Jesus Christ, I remember my heart beating a little faster. The words of life were going right into me. It was like I had never before heard the story of Jesus. Suddenly, these were not dull and meaningless words, but these were words of life sinking deep into my heart. Jesus loved not only the whole world, but He loved even me. And, He loved me so much that He died on the cross to forgive me of all my sins. The most startling truth to my young heart was the awareness that Jesus was alive. He had actually risen from the dead, and was waiting to forgive me my sins, and to fill my life with His love, peace, and joy. In a moment of time this Scripture became so clear to me:

*Behold, I stand at the door and knock. If
anyone hears My voice and opens the door, I*

*will come in to him and dine with him, and he
with Me.*
Revelation 3:20

As Betty concluded the account of Jesus' death on the cross, His burial, and His resurrection, I could actually feel His Presence all around me. Betty then asked us if we wanted to open our hearts and invite Him into our lives to be Savior and Lord. Never will I forget the pounding of my heart as I raised my hand and said: "Yes Jesus, come into my heart and life." On that blessed March night, a seeking, searching young girl, and a seeking, searching Savior met and had a personal encounter that would forever mark and determine the course of her life. C.H. Spurgeon wrote of his own conversion in these words: "I looked at Him, and He looked at me and we were one forever."

As I now look back over these many years, I marvel that on that night so long ago the Savior reached down and forever captured the heart and affections of an insecure and lonely girl, and she became His forever. How He longs to do this very same thing for all who open their hearts to Him. Of this marvelous salvation encounter Paul writes:

*. . .that if you confess with your mouth the
Lord Jesus and believe in your heart that God
has raised Him from the dead, you will be
saved. For with the heart one believes unto
righteousness, and with the mouth confession
is made unto salvation.*
Romans 10:9,10

So, throughout my journey in life it has been my joy to declare with my mouth: "Jesus, You are my Lord, Savior, Redeemer, Deliverer, Healer, and Baptizer, and with all of my heart I believe the Father has raised You from the dead and I am forever grateful for Your amazing grace and full salvation." I serve a risen Savior!

Over these many years, I have not ceased to marvel that God ever longs to capture the hearts of all of humanity. He yearns for us to open our hearts to the beauty of His love and holiness. And once we do, He will continue to thrill us and delight us with deeper and deeper insights into His Word, into His heart, and into the beauty of His ways. As the eyes of the Lord search the whole earth, have you been found?

> *For the eyes of the LORD run to and fro*
> *throughout the whole earth, to show Himself*
> *strong on behalf of those whose heart is loyal*
> *to Him.*
> II Chronicles 16:9a

Lord, here is my heart – melt me, mold me, and fill me with Your love and grace. Let my heart be forever captured by who You are. Love and win others to Yourself through my life and testimony.

RICH TOWARD GOD

. . .while you are enriched in everything for all
liberality, which causes thanksgiving through
us to God.
II Corinthians 9:11

As I was mediating in the Gospels, the parable of the rich fool from Luke 12:15-21 became especially meaningful to me.

> *And He said to them, "Take heed and beware*
> *of covetousness, for one's life does not consist*
> *in the abundance of the things he possesses."*
> *Then He spoke a parable to them, saying: "The*
> *ground of a certain rich man yielded plentifully.*
> *And he thought within himself, saying, 'What*
> *shall I do, since I have no room to store my*
> *crops?' So he said, 'I will do this: I will pull*
> *down my barns and build greater, and there I*
> *will store all my crops and my goods. And I will*
> *say to my soul, "Soul, you have many goods*
> *laid up for many years; take your ease; eat,*
> *drink, and be merry."' But God said to him,*

'Fool! This night your soul will be required of you; then whose will those things be which you have provided?' "So is he who lays up treasure for himself, and is not rich toward God."

I had been asking the Lord how the church was to prepare for the pressures of these last days. I became especially attentive to all the warnings and encouragements Jesus gave us in the Gospels. As He told the parable of the rich man, who only focuses on getting and hoarding for himself, Jesus warned:

"Take heed and beware of covetousness, for one's life does not consist in the abundance of the things he possesses."
Luke 12:15

In this parable the man's life was unexpectedly taken and the rich fool is obviously bankrupt toward God.

"So is he who lays up treasure for himself, and is not rich toward God."
Luke 12:21

The words "rich toward God" seemed to jump off the page right into my heart. "Are you rich toward Me, My child?" As I pondered these probing words, I became determined to re-evaluate my priorities and pursuits. Was I seeking first the kingdom of God, and His righteousness? Did I have increasing treasure invested in heaven?

Do not lay up for yourselves treasures on earth, where moth and rust destroy and where

*thieves break in and steal; but lay up for
yourselves treasures in heaven, where neither
moth nor rust destroys and where thieves do
not break in and steal. For where your treasure
is, there your heart will be also.*
Matthew 6:19-21

The next step in digging more deeply into what it means to be "rich towards God," was to explore what the Scripture has to say about being wealthy and rich in Him. Paul, in writing to Timothy, gives a very strong command and admonition.

*Command those who are rich in this present
age not to be haughty, nor to trust in uncertain
riches but in the living God, who gives us richly
all things to enjoy. Let them do good, that they
be rich in good works, ready to give, willing
to share, storing up for themselves a good
foundation for the time to come, that they may
lay hold on eternal life.*
I Timothy 6:17-19

From these verses it becomes obvious that cultivating a life-style of giving, sharing, and generosity is essential to becoming rich in God. We love and serve a God who longs to "richly provide us with everything for our enjoyment," so that we in turn can give and share lavishly with others. To be "rich toward God" begins with a vibrant, dynamic friendship with Him, a friendship in which we pour out our hearts to Him, a friendship in which we thoroughly enjoy His Presence, and value Him sharing His heart with us.

For much of my life I have been inspired and challenged by Moses' relationship with God. The Lord and he walked together, talked together, argued together, and obviously could not live without being together. Moses was rich in his relationship and friendship with God.

> *So the LORD spoke to Moses face to face, as a*
> *man speaks to his friend.*
> Exodus 33:11a

As I spent much time thinking about being rich in friendship with God, the Lord spoke clearly into my heart from these verses.

> *"I've loved you the way my Father has loved*
> *me. Make yourselves at home in my love. If you*
> *keep my commands, you'll remain intimately at*
> *home in my love. That's what I've done—kept*
> *my Father's commands and made myself at*
> *home in his love. I've told you these things for*
> *a purpose: that my joy might be your joy, and*
> *your joy wholly mature. This is my command:*
> *Love one another the way I loved you. This is*
> *the very best way to love. Put your life on the*
> *line for your friends. You are my friends when*
> *you do the things I command you. I'm no longer*
> *calling you servants because servants don't*
> *understand what their master is thinking and*
> *planning. No, I've named you friends because*
> *I've let you in on everything I've heard from*
> *the Father. You didn't choose me, remember;*
> *I chose you, and put you in the world to bear*
> *fruit, fruit that won't spoil. As fruit bearers,*

> *whatever you ask the Father in relation to*
> *me, he gives you. But remember the root*
> *command: Love one another."*
> John 15:9-17 The Message

In discussing this meaningful passage with the Lord, I asked that I would never be content to live merely as an acquaintance, or even as a servant, but that I would always pursue a rich friendship of intimacy with Him.

As I continued to pursue the theme of being rich in and toward God, a memory from long ago put a smile of understanding on my face. It was May, 1956, I was a senior in Grover Cleveland high school in Brooklyn, New York, and I was in the midst of writing term papers, and immersed in studying for finals. In the midst of the pressure and deadlines of being a graduating senior, I took a few minutes to rest and recline on the couch. "Hi Lord, it's me again, asking for Your help and strength in all of this." Never will I forget what happened next. Into my mind came the announcement from weeks ago (which I had forgotten all about), announcing a senior essay contest entitled: "Horizons for the 1956 Graduate." In this essay we were to include our goals and visions for the future. Quietly the impression came to me that I was to write this essay and enter the contest.

I remember groaning and saying, "Lord, how could You be asking me to do this? I have too much to do, I haven't thought about the subject, and I don't have a clue what to write about." Yet, the impression only became stronger, and with a sigh I went back to the kitchen table, pulled out some paper, put down my head and said: "OK, Lord, now what?"

Immediately an article quoting this Scripture came to mind, and with it came a rich flow of creative energy and insight.

> *"Let not the wise man glory in his wisdom,*
> *let not the mighty man glory in his might, nor*
> *let the rich man glory in his riches; but let him*
> *who glories glory in this, that he understands*
> *and knows Me, that I am the LORD, exercising*
> *loving kindness, judgment, and righteousness*
> *in the earth. For in these I delight,"*
> *says the LORD.*
> Jeremiah 9:23,24

In essence, I wrote that the graduating senior would not find his fulfillment or completion in the wisdom of education, in the physical strength of his life, nor in the accumulation of wealth and riches, but only in knowing and enjoying his creator – God. In everything else that could be achieved and accomplished in the coming years, understanding the kindness, justice, and righteousness of the Lord, who not only created us, but who also loved and saved us, brings Him great delight and us deep fulfillment. Someone who lived to bring the Lord delight would also live to bring kindness, justice, and righteousness into every aspect of his life, work, and profession. Such a person will change the future.

I still get thrilled with the memory of sitting at the small kitchen table and experiencing His Presence and inspiration as I wrote. The paper was due by 10:00 am the next morning. It still amazes me that a paper so filled with Scripture and references to God was so readily accepted by a public high school. (But then, it was 1956!) I also recall that I distinctly felt rich in God. If nothing ever resulted from writing this paper, I knew that I brought Him plea-sure by obeying and trusting Him in writing it. Yes, my family of four lived in a very small, five-room New York apartment, having limited financial resources, but that day I knew I was rich in God. It was also an experience of revelation in God that would always help chart the course of my own life.

Never will I forget graduation day, when my name was called as the winner of the senior essay contest. Not only did my parents beam with happiness, but I also won a cash prize, and had my name displayed on a poster in the local bank where my dad did all of his banking. (The Lord also used this to soften the hearts of my parents toward Himself and towards my desire to be in full time service to the Lord.)

Many years have passed since that momentous and special event, but its impact has only increased in my life. The longing to know Him in His kindness, justice, and righ-teousness, and to richly live and express those qualities to all around me is one of the strategic goals of my life. To be rich in the fruit of the Spirit, to be rich in relationships, to be rich in acts of kindness and generosity towards others, these bring delight and pleasure to Him.

As I continued to meditate on the biblical theme of being "rich toward God," another passage of Scripture came quickly to mind:

Everything that goes into a life of pleasing God has been miraculously given to us by getting to know, personally and intimately, the One who invited us to God. The best invitation we ever received! We were also given absolutely terrific promises to pass on to you— your tickets to participation in the life of God after you turned your back on a world corrupted by lust. So don't lose a minute in building on what you've been given, complementing your basic faith with good character, spiritual understanding, alert discipline, passionate patience, reverent wonder, warm friendliness, and generous love, each dimension fitting into and developing the others. With these qualities active and growing in your lives, no grass will grow under your feet; no day will pass without its reward as you mature in your experience of our Master Jesus. Without these qualities you can't see what's right before you, oblivious that your old sinful life has been wiped off the books. So, friends, confirm God's invitation to you, his choice of you. Don't put it off; do it now. Do this, and you'll have your life on a firm footing, the streets paved and the way wide open into the eternal kingdom of our Master and Savior, Jesus Christ.

2 Peter 1:3-11 The Message

From this encouraging passage it is clear that the Lord greatly values godly character. As we grow in the grace and knowledge of the Lord Jesus not only will we be enriched, but we will also enrich everyone else's life. I sense that this is something of Paul's meaning when he writes:

> *. . . as sorrowful, yet always rejoicing; as poor,*
> *yet making many rich; as having nothing, and*
> *yet possessing all things.*
> II Corinthians 6:10

Regardless of outward circumstances, we as God's people are blessed and favored with the rich Presence and deposit of God in our lives. And as Peter concluded his thoughts on making our calling and election sure, the NIV beautifully translates 2 Peter 1:11 with these words:

> *And you will receive a rich welcome*
> *into the eternal kingdom of our Lord*
> *and Savior Jesus Christ.*

In sharp contrast to the parable of the materially rich fool who entered eternity bankrupt and "not rich toward God," Peter unfolds the beauty of one who is wealthy in godly character and who is given a "rich welcome into the eternal kingdom."

Thank you, thank you, beloved Lord, for so enriching our lives. May we always be rich in character, good deeds, and lavish generosity toward others. Lord, we live to bring delight to your heart. You are the treasure of our lives.

NIAGARA'D BY HIS LOVE

*Now hope does not disappoint, because the
love of God has been poured out in our hearts
by the Holy Spirit who was given to us.*
Romans 5:5

One of my greatest sources of joy and laughter comes
from spending time with my three daughters. They
are all married, and very busy young women, but at least
once a year we try to do a girls' "get-away." These days are
all wonderfully memorable and fond times to recall.

Of all the trips, the one the four of us took to Niagara
Falls will always be a highlight for me. Through the use of
many coupons and online discounts, we were able to get
rooms that directly overlooked the Canadian Falls. The
view was breath-taking. Since the windows were large,
we pulled four chairs directly in front of them. There we
sat talking to one another while intently looking at the
splendor of the falls. As I watched the beauty and power
of the rushing water, my mind went to Romans 5:5,
"God has poured out His love into our hearts by the Holy
Spirit. . . ." The Word "poured" is comparable to the word

"Niagara'd." I excitedly quoted the verse to my daughters, and told them to imagine standing under the outpouring of these magnificent falls. Of course, because of the power of the water, no one could actually stand. Yet, such is the power of His love that He continuously desires to fill us with an unlimited supply and abundance of His life and love!

This is a love that the prophet, Jeremiah states is an everlasting love: The LORD has appeared of old to me, saying: "Yes, I have loved you with an everlasting love; therefore with lovingkindness I have drawn you" (31:3). To yield our lives to Him, and to receive His unfailing love is to experience the Spirit-filled life.

That evening we closed the drapes so that we could sleep in. But as usual, I awoke early. Not wanting to awaken Laura, I sat in one of the chairs looking at the closed drapes. Such frustration! Here I was, knowing, that if the curtain were opened, I would be viewing one of the seven wonders of the world! As I sat there in the darkness, the Lord began to speak to my heart about eternity and the unseen world. "If you could see beyond the veil of earthly things, you would be more thrilled with the beauty of the spiritual, unseen realm than anything you see on this earth." Immediately, these Scriptures came to mind:

. . .for our light affliction, which is but a moment, is working for us a far more exceeding and eternal weight of glory. . . .while we do not look at the things which are seen, but at the things which are not seen. For the things which

*are seen are temporary, but the things which
are not seen are eternal.*
II Corinthians 4:17,18

*If then you were raised with Christ, seek those
things which are above, where Christ is, sitting
at the right hand of God. Set your mind on
things above not on things on the earth.*
Colossians 3:1,2

As I continued to sit in the darkness, knowing that if the drapes were opened, the view would be a feast to my eyes, The Lord continued to speak to me of the beauty and reality of the spiritual world, and I found myself enjoying a feast for my soul from His Word. Finally, I just had to take a little peak, and as I just barely moved the drape, I heard my daughter chuckle as she said, "Mom, open the drape already." With a sweep of my hand, the room was filled with the brilliant sunshine, and the magnificent beauty of those powerful waterfalls. This was indeed a beautiful visual, even if only in small measure, of what awaits us as His children. And so it shall be in the hour of His return, and no longer will there be any darkness.

*Behold, I tell you a mystery: we shall not all
sleep, but we shall all be changed. . . .*
I Corinthians 15:51

. . .for the glory of God illuminated it. . . .
Revelation 21:23

*Eye has not seen, nor ear heard, nor have
entered into the heart of man the things which*

*God has prepared for those who love Him. But
God has revealed them to us through His Spirit.
For the spirit searches all things, yes, the deep
things of God.*
I Corinthians 2:9,10

Thank you, Father, for what You have prepared for us.
Thank you that even now You pour into us Your powerful,
healing love preparing us for the day when our faith will
be turned into sight, and we will dwell in the beauty of
Your Presence forever.

Delighting in the Word of God

Your words were found, and I ate them, and
Your word was to me the joy and rejoicing of
my heart; for I am called by Your name, O LORD
God of hosts.
Jeremiah 15:16

I still vividly remember the frustration I experienced as a young believer when I was told that for me to grow as a disciple of Jesus, I had to read, study and delight in the Word of God. Often the beauty of Psalm 1 was used and discussed as an incentive to delight in God's Word.

. . .But his delight is in the law of the LORD, and
in His law he meditates day and night. He shall
be like a tree planted by the rivers of water,
that brings forth its fruit in its season, whose
leaf also shall not wither; and whatever he
does shall prosper.
Psalm 1:2-3

However, when I was alone I soon discovered that I didn't really comprehend what it meant to delight in God's

Word. In reality, at times the Scripture seemed boring and beyond my understanding. Honestly acknowledging this also brought some intense feelings of guilt and unworthiness.

Then came the early morning of January 1954! At 5:00 A.M., as a very ill teenager, I sovereignly encountered the love of God, was filled with His Spirit, and found my life forever changed. The first evidence of His Spirit filling my life was that the Word of God became alive and relevant to me. I soon learned the powerful truth of the ministry of the Holy Spirit in leading us to love and delight in His Word:

> *"But the Helper, the Holy Spirit, whom the*
> *Father will send in My name, He will teach you*
> *all things, and bring to your remembrance all*
> *things that I said you."*
> John 14:26

The Holy Spirit is our teacher. Jesus taught us to expect Him to guide us into all Truth. What a powerful incentive to learn to dwell in His Word, and to discern His voice.

> *"However, when He, the Spirit of truth, has*
> *come, He will guide you into all truth; for*
> *He will not speak on His own authority, but*
> *whatever He hears He will speak; and He will*
> *tell you things to come."*
> John 16:13

I soon discovered that our growing, experiential knowledge of God through His Word is the food of our faith. Someone has written, "The Word of God is kindling for the 'smoking flax' of our soul." As we yield ourselves to the Holy Spirit, He opens our minds to understand the Scriptures, and causes our heart to burn in desire for Him.

> *And they said to one another, "Did not our*
> *heart burn within us while He talked with us on*
> *the road, and while He opened the Scriptures*
> *to us?"*
> Luke 24:32

During my years, especially as a single young person, I made some choices that were to determine the rest of my life. I took very seriously Paul's admonitions:

> *Be diligent to present yourself approved*
> *to God, a worker who does not need to be*
> *ashamed, rightly dividing the word of truth.*
> II Timothy 2:15

> *Let the word of Christ dwell in you*
> *richly in all wisdom, teaching and admonishing*
> *one another in psalms and hymns and spiritual*
> *songs, singing with grace in your hearts*
> *to the Lord.*
> Colossians 3:16

I decided to actively participate in as many small group Bible studies as my college schedule would allow. I also decided that wherever the Word of God was being preached and taught I would be there. Living in New York City gave me many opportunities to hear God's Word taught by seasoned servants of God. I still remember the messages brought by A.W. Tozer, Alan Redpath, Leonard Ravenhill, Stephen Olford, Betty Elliot, and many others whose lives and messages would forever mark my life.

Then there was the process of learning that to delight in His Word was often preceded by the discipline of learning to diligently and consistently study and meditate in His Word.

> *Then Jesus said to those Jews who believed*
> *Him, "If you abide in My word, you are My*
> *disciples indeed. And you shall know the truth,*
> *and the truth shall make you free."*
> John 8:31-32

Dr. F.B. Meyer, one of the most influential Bible teachers of the early 20th century was, and continues to be, one of my mentors in unfolding biblical truths to my hungry soul. Even though he is now in God's Presence, his writings on both Old and New Testament men of faith continues to teach and speak to new generations of believers. It is he who wrote: " So there are mysteries of glory and beauty in Scriptures hidden from the wise and prudent, but revealed to babes. There is no book that will so repay time spent over its pages as the Word of God."

Every serious disciple of Jesus will want to make a commitment to read through the Scriptures from Genesis to Revelation as often as possible. (There are many "reading through the Bible" plans available) It is also very inspiring to read through whole books of the Bible either in one sitting or in one week (depending on the length of the book). Then there are times when we will want to simply concentrate on one psalm, or one verse upon which to meditate. Often I find myself involved in many different disciplines of study and meditation at the same time. No wonder David could find such life and hope in God's Word.

Open my eyes that I may see wonderful things
in your law.
Psalm 119:18 NIV

. . .for I delight in your commands
because I love them.
Psalm 119:47 NIV

Oh, how I love your law!
I meditate on it all day long.
Psalm 119:97 NIV

Your statutes are wonderful;
therefore I obey them.
Psalm 119:129 NIV

The unfolding of your words gives light; it gives
understanding to the simple.
Psalm 119:130 NIV

Even in the midst of much trouble and testing, Job wrote these powerful words:

I have not departed from the commandment
of His lips; I have treasured the words of His
mouth more than my necessary food.
Job 23:12

43

It is essential to gain as much information and knowledge of Scripture as possible, but it is only as we deeply meditate in the Word, and invite the Holy Spirit to reveal and illuminate to us the beauty of Jesus in it, that we are changed and transformed. The essential key to the transformation is obedience! For it is in obedience to God's Word, and not just information about it, that will always determine our depth of revelation into His heart and His ways.

> *But be doers of the word, and not hearers only,*
> *deceiving yourselves.*
> James 1:22

As we continue to hunger and thirst for the glory of His Presence, He invites us into the deeper places of the revelation of His Word. In preparation for these momentous days in which we live, God's clear call is for us to be radically passionate about being people both of the Spirit and of the Truth.

Lord, deliver us from shallow roots and superficial fruit. Draw us into Your heart and let the aroma of Your extravagant lavish love and mercy fill us and flow through us. Jesus we love You, and delight in our growing knowledge of You and of Your Word.

BE SERIOUS, HAVE A STRATEGY
By Dianna Schmitt Whittle

*"These are the very Scriptures that testify
about me" —Jesus Christ*
John 5:39 NIV

"We come to Scripture not to learn a subject
but to steep ourselves in a person."
—C. S. Lewis

A number of years ago, I woke up one day and realized that I was unhappy with my spiritual growth. In the natural I was maturing, but spiritually and emotionally I was not making the progress that I wanted. Life experiences had taught me that even though a person may physically mature, they can nevertheless remain emotionally stuck and spiritually immature. Decades may pass and yet no real depth of character is developed within a person. The thought of that sobered me into taking immediate action.

Despite being a pastor's kid, growing up in the church, walking with the Lord for three decades, and serving full time on the church staff, I still found myself at times barely moving forward. Instead of running fully focused, often I fell back into simply puttering around the laps of life with little drive or direction. I made a choice in my heart that very day that I would "train myself to be godly" as Paul admonished Timothy, his spiritual son and co-laborer, in 1 Timothy 4:7. The truth is that each of us will one day cross the finish line of life. Some will have intentionally developed stamina through spiritual training and end with great honor, while others will practically crawl to the finish line due to their anemic condition. I wondered if I would be able to declare with humble confidence as did Paul in 2 Timothy 4:7, "I have fought the good fight; I have finished the race; I have kept the faith." "Yes, I will!" I declared to myself out loud. My hope-filled confidence came from a promise in the Scriptures, "that he who began a good work in me will carry it on to completion until the day of Christ Jesus" (Philippians 1:6). My Lord is willing, now I must choose to align myself with Him.

From that day forward, I decided to "be serious and walk out a strategy." First, I had to acknowledge that I can do nothing in my own strength. The most foundational step in spiritual growth is completely relying upon the life of Jesus within me. Galatians 2:20 is a fundamental Scripture in the Christian walk:

I have been crucified with Christ and I no longer live, but Christ lives in me. The life I live in the body, I live by the faith of the Son of God, who loved me and gave himself for me.

In the margin of my Bible I wrote, "This verse guarantees a 100% promise of change in my life." This promise in Galatians echoes the truth from which I have gained tremendous strength over the years:

> *. . . not by might, nor by power, but by My*
> *Spirit, says the Lord.*
> Zechariah 4:6

What is the life of Christ within us? Jesus Himself addressed this in John 15:4-5 (NIV) when He said:

> *Remain in me, and I will remain in you. No*
> *branch can bear fruit by itself; it must remain*
> *in the Vine. Neither can you bear fruit unless*
> *you remain in me. I am the Vine; you are the*
> *branches. If a man remains in me and I in him,*
> *he will bear much fruit; apart from me you can*
> *do nothing.*

Have you ever asked how verses like Galatians 2:20 and John 15:4-5 become a reality? I sure have! And I have good news for you. Paul declares in Philippians 2:13 (Living Bible):

> *For God is at work within you, helping you to*
> *want to obey him and then helping you do*
> *what he wants.*

The reality is, Jesus Christ in me is the hope of glory (Colossians 1:27)! In my daily life as a Christian, the most important key to my strength and growth is relying completely on the power of Jesus Christ within me. I acknowledge with my heart, my mind, and my mouth that it is in Him that I live and move and have my being (Acts 17:28)! That is the truth, regardless of whether I feel it all the time or not. Secondly, I had to use the next essential key to my spiritual growth, feeding continuously on the Word of God.

> *All Scripture is God-breathed and is useful for teaching, rebuking, correcting and training in righteousness, so that the man of God may be thoroughly equipped for every good work.*
> 2 Timothy 3:16,17 NIV

By applying the Word to my life, I was promised that I would enrich my life with wisdom, adjustment, and direction. Colossians 3:16 urges us to, "Let the Word of Christ dwell in you richly." In the Living Bible it is translated this way, "Remember what Christ taught you and let His words enrich your lives and make you wise." Jesus said:

> *If you hold to my teaching, you are really my disciples. Then you will know the truth and the truth will set you free.*
> John 8:31-32 NIV

Stop for a moment and think about that with me. How can I "hold to His teachings" if I do not know what they are? I must learn His teachings, hold to His teachings, and then just as He promised, I will know the Truth and the Truth will set me free! In Romans 12:2, Paul boldly challenges us:

*Do not conform any longer to the patterns of
this world, but be transformed by the renewing
of your mind.*

This transformation comes from continually washing my mind with the water of His Word. I was not content to simply be different on the surface, but I yearned to be transformed deep within where character is developed. The secret issues of my heart needed a transformation into the likeness of Jesus. These were issues of integrity, honor, humility, honesty, patience, forgiveness, etc. For genuine spiritual maturity, I realized that I must choose to be transformed through the daily washing of the Word of God. The author of Hebrews reminded me that:

*The Word of God is alive and active. Sharper
than any double-edged sword, it penetrates
even to dividing soul and spirit, joints and
marrow; it judges (exposes) the thoughts and
attitudes of the heart. (4:12)*

The writer of Psalm 119 took me back to the priceless gems that I was taught to memorize and sing as young child in Sunday school: "I have hidden Your Word in my heart that I might not sin against you" (v. 11 NIV), and "Your Word is a lamp to my feet and a light to my path" (v. 105 NIV).

As I come to diligently study the Scriptures, I do not find salvation in them without believing that Jesus Christ is God's Son, sent to be the Savior of the world. For Jesus said to the religious unbelievers of His day:

"You study the Scriptures diligently because you think that in them you have eternal life. These are the very Scriptures that testify about me, yet you refuse to come to me to have life."
John 5:38-40 NIV

Remembering the words of C.S. Lewis, "we come to the Scriptures not to study a subject, but to steep ourselves in a Person." John 1:1-2 pronounces that, "In the beginning was the Word, and the Word was with God, and the Word was God. The same was in the beginning with God." Romans 9:5 boldly declares that Jesus "Christ is God over all. . . ." Jesus is the Word, and the Word testifies of Him. That is Who I seek.

It is time to be serious and to have a strategy. First of all, I encourage you to pray for yourself. Talk to your Heavenly Father all throughout your day. Ask Him for help. Pray Psalm 119:18 over yourself: "Open my eyes that I may see the wonderful things in your law."

Next, choose to make a renewed commitment of your will to get into the Word of God every day. Here are but a few suggestions to assist you in developing your own strategy.

- Set the Scriptures playing continually throughout your home and in your car.

- Listen to Scripture on MP3 Player or iPod as you cook, wash dishes, fold laundry, rake leaves, etc. Personally, I have found that listening to the Bible can be a great preventative against complaining about my chores.

- Carry memory verses in your bag and diligently read them both silently and aloud. To memorize them, read the verse out loud a few times, then close your eyes and practice one phrase at a time. Repeat this over a number of days until the entire verse is committed to memory. Practice this regularly and you will find that in no time you will have hidden His Word in your heart.

- Always carry a Bible in your car. You never know when you will be delayed at the doctor's office, at football practice, waiting for a prescription, etc.

- Print out specific chapters of the Bible in very large print to read while walking on the treadmill or exercise machine (biblegateway.com is an excellent resource).

- Have an accountability partner, someone who cares enough about you to check in with you about your spiritual walk and daily Bible reading.

- When you fall behind, get up again, for Scripture promises that if we fall, we will not be hurled headlong because it is God who holds our hand. (Psalm 37:24 NASB).

His promise to you is that as you steep yourself in Him through saturating yourself in His Word, you will know the Truth and the Truth will set you free. Now be richly blessed as you get serious and have a strategy!

Heavenly Father, thank You for the promise that it is You at work within me, helping me to want to obey You, and then helping me do what You want (Philippians 2:13). I ask You to unfold a deep desire within my heart to meditate daily in Your Word. Open my eyes that I may see the wonderful things in your law (Psalm 119:18). In the precious Name of the Lord Jesus Christ I pray, Amen.

A DEFINING QUESTION

He said to them, "But who do you say
that I am?"
Matthew 16:15

*P*erhaps because I have always learned primarily by
asking questions, the questions Jesus asked have
always greatly challenged me. Jesus loves to ask us questions, and how we answer His questions will determine
how we live both here and in eternity. Of the many questions Jesus asked in the Gospels, one is absolutely strategic and life-determining: "Who do you say that I am?"

Matthew 16 is a riveting account of Jesus' interaction
with His disciples. After seemingly endless heated discussions with the religious people of His day, Jesus took
His disciples up north to a strategic place called Caesarea
Philippi. Not only would they have more private time
there, but it was also where some of the Old Testament
kings erected high altars to other gods. How very appro-
priate that in this place of idolatry, Jesus should bring
His disciples to a point of clarity as to His own identity.
The question was asked, "Who do people say that I am?"

(Matthew 16:13) As is also true today, people had many different opinions as to the true identity of Jesus Christ.

This question became extremely personal and critical to me during my college days. Since I was a philosophy major at Queens College in New York City, part of our studies were to teach us to be critical and analytic thinkers. As we studied all the major philosophers, and religious philosophies, everything I had ever been taught as a Christian was severely challenged. It was a scary and dark time for me. I questioned everything and everyone, but early in my Christian journey I had made two commitments which kept me during those turbulent times of questionings and doubts. First, I had made a commitment to read the Scriptures each day (regardless of how "dry" and "irrelevant" they felt at times), and I also made a commitment to stay connected with the family of God (regardless of how they annoyed me at times). These two choices would eventually yield some wonderful results.

It was during this dark season that Jesus' question, "Who do you say I am?" pierced my own heart. Was He just another great moral teacher, a mere man who did and taught wonderful things? Was He equal to Mohammed, Buddha, Confucius? Was He just one of many ways to God? My personal three-year journey exploring these questions could fill another book, but with great clarity and joy I still remember reading 1 John while riding the Flushing Avenue bus into Queens. The honest questions and probing of my own heart and mind were divinely answered by the Lord of Lords Himself through the revelations of His Word to my heart. I read:

Beloved, do not believe every spirit, but test the
spirits, whether they are of God; because many
false prophets have gone out into the world.
By this you know the Spirit of God: every spirit
that confesses that Jesus Christ has come in the
flesh is of God. . . .
1 John 4:1,2

Sitting in the bus that fall morning, a shaft of light and revelation pierced my heart. "My daughter, if there were any other way for man to be reconciled to Me, I would not have sent My Son. All of religion is man trying to reach Me, but when I sent Jesus, it was Me reaching down to man. From now on you will evaluate everything you study as to how it relates to My revealed truth in Christ." How clearly I recall the liberating freedom of truth when I understood as never before Jesus' words:

Then Jesus said to those Jews who believed
Him, "If you abide in My word, you are My
disciples indeed. And you shall know the truth,
and the truth shall make you free."
John 8:31,32

How I could relate to Peter's response to Jesus' question: "Who do *you* say I am?" "You are the Christ, the Son of the living God." I sensed there was great joy in Jesus as He responded:

Jesus answered and said to him, "Blessed are
you, Simon Bar-Jonah, for flesh and blood has

*not revealed this to you, but My Father who is
in heaven."*
Matthew 16:17

The key word is "revealed". It was the Holy Spirit who took the veil from Peter's eyes so he could recognize Jesus as the long-awaited Messiah, the Son of the living God.

The next couple of years in the philosophy department were some of the most meaningful in my Christian journey. I was amazed by how desirous Jesus is to always reveal Himself as the Way, the Truth, and the Life in the midst of all of the seeming wisdom of the world. I spent much time considering Paul's words in I Corinthians 1 and 2.

*. . .lest anyone should say that I had baptized
in my own name. Yes, I also baptized the
household of Stephanas. Besides, I do not know
whether I baptized any other. For Christ did not
send me to baptize, but to preach the gospel,
not with wisdom of words, lest the cross of
Christ should be made of no effect. For the
message of the cross is foolishness to those
who are perishing, but to us who are being
saved it is the power of God. For it is written: "I
will destroy the wisdom of the wise, and bring
to nothing the understanding of the prudent."
Where is the wise? Where is the scribe? Where
is the disputer of this age? Has not God made
foolish the wisdom of this world? . . .but we
preach Christ crucified, to the Jews a stumbling
block and to the Greeks foolishness, but to*

those who are called, both Jews and Greeks,
Christ the power of God and
the wisdom of God.
I Corinthians 1:15-20,23,24

To know, love, and obey Jesus is to be taken into the profound places of God's wisdom and truth. According to Paul, God has a secret wisdom in Christ which is revealed to us by His Holy Spirit.

But as it is written: Eye has not seen, nor ear
heard, nor have entered into the heart of man
the things which God has prepared for those
who love Him. But God has revealed them to
us through His Spirit. For the Spirit searches all
things, yes, the deep things of God.
1 Corinthians 2:9,10

Learning the deep things of God is open to every seeking, thirsty, and hungry pursuer of God, and they are always discovered in a greater revelation of the beauty of the Person and work of Jesus. He alone is the Author and Finisher of our faith. During these many years, study and meditation in the book of John has continued to be life-changing.

Vividly, I recall sitting in a philosophy class where we were discussing the concepts of being, essence, and life. In the midst of a lively discussion, our professor gave us one of the best examples of the meaning of essence. "Some-place in the Old Testament Moses was discussing the fact that all the surrounding people had gods with names, so Moses asked his God, what is your name? To which he received the answer, 'I am, that I am' is my name. In the Hebrew this is an excellent unfolding of the meaning of the word 'being,' or 'essence.' By the way, this same word was used by Jesus in the New Testament. In an argument with the religious order of His day, Jesus states, 'Before Abraham was, I am.'" Our professor continued with his lecture, but I sat there rather stunned and excited. Had anyone heard what he had just said? Sitting there I pulled out my small Bible, which I had learned to always carry with me, and turned to the two portions of Scripture to which he had referred. Exodus 3:12-15 is one of the most profound Scriptures of the Old Testament. It is there that Jesus revealed His unique covenant and holy name of Jehovah or Yahweh: "I am who I am." He was telling Moses, I am Essence; personal, continuous, absolute Existence, and pure Being. The other Scripture I found in John 8:58. Reading the whole context of the discussion between Jesus and the religious leaders was absolutely riveting. In discussing Abraham, Jesus states:

> *"Your father Abraham rejoiced to see My day,*
> *and he saw it and was glad." Then the Jews*
> *said to Him, "You are not yet fifty years old,*
> *and have You seen Abraham?" Jesus said to*
> *them, "Most assuredly, I say to you, before*
> *Abraham was, I AM."*
> John 8:56-58

The word for "I am" in the Greek is the same word for "I am" in the Hebrew in Exodus 3. I could hardly wait for class to end. Since many of the students in the class were pre-rabbinical students, and since we had developed a good rapport over the couple of years we were together in the philosophy department, I felt very comfortable in issuing this challenge. "Hey, did you hear what the professor said? After some discussion I felt led to challenge them that to be intellectually and academically honest they could not reject something before giving it an honest examination. So began an informal investigation of the New Testament document of the Gospel of John, each Friday at 3:00 pm in the cafeteria.

This experience also began some of the most exciting and challenging months of my college career. At one "investigation" study, led by a very bright Jewish student, the Holy Spirit unveiled Jesus in a powerful way. We were all over the New Testament documents in that study. Somehow we landed in the book of Romans. Eddie began to read:

> *Therefore we were buried with Him through*
> *baptism into death, that just as Christ was*
> *raised from the dead by the glory of the Father,*
> *even so we also should walk in newness of life.*
> Romans 6:4

The room became absolutely still as the Holy Spirit began to zero in on Eddie's heart. He actually looked a little pale to us as he laid down the Bible and exclaimed, "O my God, He's alive!" None of us stirred as Eddie, stunned, walked into the next room. After a few minutes three of us who had known him and been praying for him walked into the room. He looked at us with tears in his eyes. I remember asking Eddie what had happened to him, to which he responded "I don't really know, but as I read, ". . .just as Christ was raised from the dead. . . "I know

He's alive. What happened to me?" The three of us just looked at him in wonder, "Why Eddie, the Messiah has just revealed Himself to you." So, as to Peter and to countless others in every generation since, this same precious, beautiful, magnificent, great I AM of all the ages continues to ask: "Who do you say that I am?" How we answer this question will determine the course of our earthly life and our destiny for all eternity!

Thank you, Holy Spirit, for revealing Jesus to us. To know You, Jesus, is to love You. Thank you, Father, that throughout our lives the Holy Spirit continues to bring us to deeper places of revelation and understanding of the rich treasure that is found in the Son of God, Jesus, the great "I AM."

> *"Do not be afraid; I am the First and the Last.*
> *I am He who lives, and was dead, and behold,*
> *I am alive forevermore. Amen. And I have the*
> *keys of Hades and of Death."*
> Revelation 1:17c,18

Do I Really Love Him?

*Jesus said to him, "'You shall love the LORD
your God with all your heart, with all your soul,
and with all your mind.' This is the first and
great commandment."*
Matthew 22:37,38

*B*iographies of great men and women of God
have always inspired me. As a teenager I can still
remember the impact that these true accounts of those
who passionately served and obeyed the Lord made on
my life. Lovers of God, such as Hudson Taylor, C. T. Studd,
Amy Carmichael, Rees Howell, George Mueller, and Kath-
erine Booth were only some whose lives encouraged and
strengthened the resolve of my young heart to love and
serve Him.

Soon it was the biographies in Scripture that captivated
my mind and heart. I have learned much from Peter's life.
Sometimes the people the Lord chose to be His followers
make me smile, wonder, and receive great encouragement from. It would seem as if He can only use failures to
be His choice servants.

Peter is a prime example of someone who really didn't know the fickleness and duplicity of his own heart. He was as shifting sand in his personality. One moment he was the recipient of divine revelation causing Him to boldly acknowledge "You are the Christ, the Son of the living God" (Matthew 16:16). The next minute he was being strongly rebuked by the Lord for interfering with God's purposes:

> *". . .you do not have in mind the things of God,*
> *but the things of men."*
> Matthew 16:23 NIV

Even on the mountain where Jesus was actually trans-figured before his eyes, Peter seemed to be missing the point. He was rambling on to the extent that God the Father Himself interrupted him:

> *While he was still speaking,*
> *behold, a bright cloud overshadowed them;*
> *and suddenly a voice came out of the cloud,*
> *saying, "This is My beloved Son, in whom I am*
> *well pleased. Hear Him!"*
> Matthew 17:5

Who can read the precious account of Jesus and His disciples in John 13 without experiencing a smile, a tear, and a fear? As Jesus was pouring out His heart to them, telling them of His upcoming death and departure and the need for them to deeply love one another, Peter again demonstrated his complete ignorance of what his own heart was capable of:

Peter said to Him, "Lord, why can I not follow You now? I will lay down my life for Your sake."
John 13:37

I can only imagine his shock when Jesus looked at him and answered:

"Will you lay down your life for My sake? Most assuredly, I say to you, the rooster shall not crow till you have denied Me three times."
John 13:38

Oh, the turmoil of those last days before Jesus was crucified! Each disciple would be tested and tried to the breaking point, but none quite like Peter. The patience and persistence of Jesus in His dealing with and training of those who would serve Him is absolutely amazing to observe.

At the last supper, after which the very conflict of the ages was to be played out both in Gethsemane and Calvary, the disciples were still so dull of understanding that Luke records that they were actually arguing about which of them would be considered the greatest. I imagine that Peter took the lead in this argument because Jesus spoke specifically to him:

And the Lord said, "Simon, Simon! Indeed, Satan has asked for you, that he may sift you as wheat."
Luke 22:31

This brief verse tells us that Jesus is praying for us. Indeed, we are always on His prayer list. What an encouragement!

> *Therefore He is also able to save to the*
> *uttermost those who come to God through*
> *Him, since He always lives to make intercession*
> *for them.*
> Hebrews 7:25

Even though Jesus spoke this profound prophetic statement to Peter, he once again completely missed the point:

> *But he said to Him, Lord, I am ready to go with*
> *You, both to prison and to death.*
> Luke 22:33

Next, the greatest trauma of Peter's life occurred. Luke records these events in chapter 22. After Jesus' arrest, Peter cowered in fear and intimidation before some servant girls, and three times adamantly denied that he even knew Jesus. Some translations suggest that his denial was filled with curses and expletives! In this painful and riveting account, Luke wrote:

> *Immediately, while he was still speaking,*
> *the rooster crowed. And the Lord turned and*
> *looked at Peter. Then Peter remembered the*
> *word of the Lord, how He had said to him,*
> *"Before the rooster crows you will deny Me*
> *three times." So Peter went out*
> *and wept bitterly.*
> Luke 22: 60b-62

Jesus looked straight at Peter. I have often wondered what Peter saw in those eyes. After all, none of this caught Jesus by surprise, but He knew that Peter had to see sin and duplicity in his own heart before he could become God's anointed, bold mouthpiece.

What were those following days and nights like for Peter? I can only imagine the guilt and torment he was feeling. Peter really thought he loved Jesus. He actually thought he would stand with Him in death. It soon became obvious that Peter's confidence in himself was his greatest hindrance to fully being used for kingdom purposes. As those hours of deep anguish over what he had done accomplished its work of deep brokenness, contriteness, and humility. Peter was made ready for the Master's direct and liberating intervention.

From the account found in John 21, it is obvious that Peter's disillusionment in himself was still not fully resolved. Even after Jesus' resurrection, Peter and some of the disciples went back to Galilee to go fishing. This is rather incredible! After all, the whole destiny of the early church was on their shoulders; why would they go back to fishing at such a strategic time?

I can only imagine that in the midst of such tumultuous events, Peter sought for something familiar that he knew he could do, fishing. He was obviously a great failure and disappointment to himself, and especially to His Lord. Peter would now dramatically learn some things about his Lord that would forever change the way he thought, spoke, and lived. God is always at work in the midst of our failures, disappointments, sorrows, and confusion. He is always waiting to give us another opportunity to fulfill His purposes. He is always ready to give us some very surprising, healing encounters with Himself.

Peter was to learn that day on the Sea of Galilee that he could not even succeed at the job he knew how best to do. As the dawn appeared on the horizon, a familiar voice called out to them:

"Friends, haven't you any fish?"
John 21:5 NIV

Then a command to throw the net over the other side of the boat came to them. What a powerful memory Jesus was bringing back, especially to his dejected servant, Peter. Three and a half years before, Peter and the disciples had a similar experience which yielded spectacular results (Luke 5). And now it was happening again, and with it came the recognition by John: "It is the Lord!"

Peter, the first to come ashore, was confronted with another memory, a fire of burning coals. Yes, he had to face the place of his greatest failure in order to find healing. He then experienced even more deeply the amazing grace and love of His Master. Instead of stern rebukes and corrections, Peter finds Jesus cooking breakfast for them. How totally extraordinary was this – a God who cooked breakfast for His exhausted, confused, and faltering followers! Then Peter would be asked the most critical question of his whole life:

"Simon, son of John, do you love Me?"
John 21:17 NIV

At one time Peter with great confidence would have boasted, "Of course I love You." But now, having been shaken to his very core by his dismal failure, Peter could only say:

> *"Lord, you know all things;*
> *you know that I love you."*
> John 21:17b NIV

Greek scholars point out that different words for love were being used in this interaction between Jesus and Peter, which reveals that Peter wasn't as certain as he was before concerning the unconditional nature of his love for Jesus. Yet, that love would eventually work itself into the very fabric of his being, but for now, Peter knew he had a deep abiding affection for Jesus. Yes, Peter did love Jesus. Of all the questions Jesus could ask, "Do you love Me?" is the defining question not only for Peter, but for each of us. Only out of the love relationship between Jesus and His followers can the mission of the Church even be fulfilled. One can easily experience "compassion fatigue" in serving other people. It is only as we learn to enjoy His love for us, and as we learn to delight in loving Him with all our heart, mind, soul, and strength, that we are then equipped to serve Him and fulfill His call in our lives.

In seven weeks, Peter would be filled with the Holy Spirit and preach his boldest sermon ever. For the remainder of his life Peter would prove to be a very dangerous man to the enemy and a most dynamic man of purpose, prayer, and proclamation for the kingdom of God. This transformation all took place in the cocoon of God's dealings, in which Peter had a dynamic encounter with the powerful and relentless outpouring of God's love and affection for him.

From this deepening love relationship with Jesus, I believe Peter heard often the words: "Peter, do you love Me?" Then in a humble confidence Peter could respond: "Yes, Lord, with all my heart and soul I love You." Listen to his words written almost thirty years later:

> *. . .whom having not seen you love. Though now you do not see Him, yet believing, you rejoice with joy inexpressible and full of glory. . . .*
> 1 Peter 1:8

The same question comes to each of us as His final word to us, "Son, daughter, do you love Me?"

Thank you, Jesus, for Your relentless pursuit of us. Thank you, that even in our most serious places of failure, Your love never lets us go. Thank you for Jeremiah's words, "The Lord appeared to us in the past, saying: 'I have loved you with an everlasting love; I have drawn you with unfailing kindness'" (31:3).

THE POWER OF SILENCE

"But the Lord is in His holy temple. Let all the earth keep silence before Him."
Habakkuk 2:20

". . .come aside by yourselves to a deserted place and rest a while."
Mark 6:31b

*T*hose moments around the lunch table on that hot August afternoon in the mid–70s would become life–shaping for me. A small group of us, all fairly young, enthusiastic, and quite impressed with our own level of knowledge and anointing, excitedly sat with real patriarchs of the faith, Richard and Sabina Wurmbrand. Both were Romanian Jewish believers in Yeshua. Brother Richard was also an ordained Lutheran pastor and had spent 14 years in prison, four of which were in total silence and solitary confinement. They both carried a Presence of a quiet strength and dignity about them. As we were enthusiastically sharing on the latest theological developments in the current charismatic outpouring, I observed how quietly both Brother Richard and Sister Sabina were sitting and observing. Realizing how much we all seemed to be enjoying our own opinions and evaluations, it struck me that we had two of God's treasures sitting quietly and saying nothing. Something was wrong with this picture.

Finally, we slowed down our own astute observations, and focused on our honored guests. I remember blurting out, "Brother Wurmbrand, what one thing would you want to share with those of us who are young in the ministry?" He just looked at each of us for what felt like a very long time. It took a lot of self-control for us not to begin another conversation. Finally he answered: "The power of silence." I can still remember thinking, what in the world is he talking about? How could silence be the most important lesson for us to learn? I remember walking back to the campground and expressing my frustration to Charles. How little we knew at that time of the value of quiet and silent waiting in the Presence of the Lord.

During the next days with our honored guests, things were shared and imparted to us that would permanently change our lives. Brother Richard and Sister Sabina knew God in a deep and profound way. They attributed this treasure to the power of suffering and silence in their lives. Especially when one is young, the themes of suffering and silence seem to be secondary to the exciting themes of triumph, prosperity, and victorious living, all of which are important, but only a part of the whole of Christian life.

In the months and years ahead, the power of silence and solitude began to shape how I lived my life both in public and especially in private. Learning to be quiet and silent before the Lord became essential in going from the superficial to the deeper places with God. In the midst of much external noise and upheaval, David wrote:

"Be still, and know that I am God;
I will be exalted among the nations.
I will be exalted in the earth."
Psalm 46:10

In studying the life of Jesus, I quickly learned that He clearly lived from a place of heart solitude. Jesus repeatedly calls us to that same place of quiet and rest. A study of the Gospels shows us Jesus abiding in a place of solitude and quietly soaking in His Father's love and Presence.

"Come to Me, all you who labor and are heavy
laden, and I will give you rest."
Matthew 11:28

Frequently, we find Him retreating to the quiet places:

When Jesus heard it, he departed from there
by boat to a deserted place by Himself. . . .and
when He had sent the multitudes away, He
went up on the mountain by Himself to pray.
Now when evening came, He was alone there.
Matthew 14:13a,23

It is as we cultivate a daily time of solitude and soaking in His loving Presence that the Holy Spirit opens to us the rich treasures of His heart. Outward silence is certainly easier to attain to than is a deep inner place of quiet and stillness. This place of inner quiet is a prerequisite to hearing the voice of our God. How beautifully we learn this from the life of Elijah. The Lord came to him not in the earthquakes, not in the fire, but in a "gentle whisper" (1 Kings 19). Often His word comes to us gently, quietly, and almost imperceptibly, except if we have ears to hear and eyes to see.

Learning to share with the Lord everything and anything that would cause us to have "inner noise," and even writing down those thoughts, helps to bring us to a place of inner quiet. Playing quiet worship music, welcoming His Presence, deeply breathing in His love, and speaking the beautiful name of Jesus as an expression of our love and adoration to Him draws His Presence. Learning to sit in worshipful silence with an attentive listening ear, causes our roots to go down deep into the soil of His love. Often this becomes a time of rich communion with Him and precious revelation from His Word.

As we learn to cultivate a place of silence and inner solitude, a longing for more of His Presence begins to fill our hearts. A greater hunger and thirst for His Presence takes us to yet deeper places of abiding in Him and loving obedience to Him. We soon find that we become more aware of Him in all that we think, do, and say. We are assured that He who sees in secret, shall indeed reward us openly with more of Himself. Listen to the cries of David's heart:

As the deer pants for the water brooks, so
pants my soul for You, O God. My soul thirsts
for God, for the living God. When shall I come
and appear before God?
Psalm 42:1-2

*O God, You are my God; early will I seek You;
my soul thirsts for You; my flesh longs for You in
a dry and thirsty land where there is no water.*
Psalm 63:1

Quietly meditating on His Word and feasting on the beauty of His promises strengthens and encourages our souls. As we study to be quiet and learn to stay in His healing Presence, a river of life and joy will flow into us, transforming us and those whose lives we touch. All of this comes from our private encounters with God in the secret place.

*You are my hiding place; You shall preserve me
from trouble; You shall surround me with songs
of deliverance. Selah I will instruct you and
teach you in the way you should go; I will guide
you with My eye.*
Psalm 32:7,8

Spending that one week with the Wurmbrands taught us many life-changing truths on the power of joyful suffering and faithful serving. Those significant days also taught us how to dig treasure from the secret places of His heart. Even today I smile at the memory of all that was imparted to us as young, eager servants of the Lord.

Father thank You for Your continuous invitation to meet You in the healing quiet of the secret place. And thank you that we are learning that our soul finds rest in You alone. Lord, help us to experience deeply the truth that our public ministry is no greater than our personal, secret times of intimacy with You.

*For more information about the Wurmbrands, please see http://www.womenofchristianity.com/?p=4323

LAP CLIMBING TIME

*"Can a mother forget the baby at her breast
and have no compassion on the child she has
borne? Though she may forget, I will not forget
you! See, I have engraved you on the palms of
my hands; your walls are ever before me."*
Isaiah 49:15,16 NIV

*C*an you remember back to a time in your childhood when all you wanted was the comfort of climbing onto the lap of Mom or Dad, and have them just hold you? If you have walked with the Lord for any period of time at all, you will have quickly learned that to be a Christian is certainly not all smiles, fun, and excitement. There are also seasons of tears, sorrows, and determined walking. And no matter how old you become as a believer, you will always have your "lap-climbing times"; times when you just want to be wrapped in the comfort of our Father's love.

*The eternal God is your refuge, and underneath
are the everlasting arms.*
Deuteronomy 33:27a

"He will feed His flock like a shepherd;
He will gather the lambs with His arms."
Isaiah 40:11a

Bless God for those experiences which shut us in only to Him. If we are to know any of the deep, abiding joys of intimate communion with Him in the secret places, He will have to strip us of all other man-made props and support systems. But, oh how painful such pruning of the Lord can be! How sharp His knife does appear at times! But, when our hearts have truly been captured by Him who is the fairest among ten thousand, no price will be too great to pay in order to know Him better.

One day a number of years ago, when I felt as if every fiber in my inner being was crying out in pain, I sat weeping in our big white chair in the bedroom. As I sat in the healing silence of our home, I looked up to Him and cried, "Dad, it's lap-climbing time! No one else has the balm for my heart. No one else has the wisdom for my situation right now. You've never failed me over the years, and now I need the comfort of Your Presence more than anything else."

In the stillness of the next few moments, I knew in as profound a way as I had ever known, that He was uniquely the Wonderful Counselor, the Mighty God, the Eternal Father, and the Prince of Peace (Isaiah 9:6b), and my spirit cried, "Abba Daddy!"

In his letter to the Romans Paul makes some deeply moving observations concerning our God:

*For as many as are led by
the Spirit of God, these are sons of God.
For you did not receive the spirit of bondage
again to fear, but you received the Spirit of
adoption by whom we cry out, "Abba, Father."
The Spirit Himself bears witness with our spirit
that we are children of God. . . .*
Romans 8:14-16.

For those of us who have opened up our hearts to Him, He is not only our Savior and Lord, but He is our "Abba Daddy." And He enjoys this special relationship of Papa and child perhaps more than any other. In teaching His disciples how to pray, Jesus began with this profound truth: "Our Father in heaven. . . ." As our Daddy, He Himself created us with a deep need and desire to be loved, accepted, and valued. He created us to be cherished and enjoyed. How good to saturate ourselves in the beautiful truths about our Father God!

*As a father pities his children, so the LORD
pities those who fear Him. . . . Psalm 103:13
But now, O LORD, You are our Father; we are
the clay, and You our potter; And all we are the
work of Your hand.*
Isaiah 64:8

*If you then, being evil, know how to give good
gifts to your children, how much more will your
Father who is in heaven give good things to
those who ask Him!*
Matthew 7:11

And because you are sons, God has sent forth the Spirit of His Son into your hearts, crying out, "Abba, Father!"
Galatians 4:6

". . .for the Father Himself loves you, because you have loved Me, and have believed that I came forth from God."
John 16:27

Blessed be the God and Father of our Lord Jesus Christ, the Father of mercies and God of all comfort, who comforts us in all our tribulation, that we may be able to comfort those who are in any trouble, with the comfort with which we ourselves are comforted by God.
II Corinthians 1:3-4

As I sat in my big white chair, those many, many years ago, tears running down my face, He reached down and by His Spirit brought comfort to my broken heart. I felt as if I had simply climbed up on the lap of my Heavenly Daddy, and let Him love and comfort me. As always His Spirit spoke into my spirit through His Word.

This is my comfort in my affliction, for Your word has given me life.
Psalm 119:50

Let, I pray, Your merciful kindness be for my comfort, according to Your servant.
Psalm 119:76

Thank you, Lord, for Your everlasting and unconditional love for us, and let us never forget that You are always ready waiting to give us a Daddy's hug. And thank you that Your Word always speaks life and comfort into our lives. Holy Spirit, we welcome You once again into our lives as the great Comforter of our souls.

PAINFUL MYSTERIES

These all died in faith, not having received the promises, but having seen them afar off were assured of them, embraced them and confessed that they were strangers and pilgrims on the earth.
Hebrews 11:13

*H*ow could she have died? There was so much faith in her heart and in the atmosphere around her. "Lord, what went wrong?" My heart was in anguish over Betty's death. She was too young to die. She had too many unfinished dreams. Betty was not only a devoted wife and mother, but she was also my administrative assistant for eight years. She was an excellent ministry traveling companion and dear friend. Her journey from health, to sickness, to death, went very quickly, but weren't we as a faith community believing and standing on His promises?

As I was once again painfully pondering, "when God doesn't make sense" issues, my heart cried out for some answers. Early in my Christian walk, I had been encouraged to ask the hard questions of the Lord. The Lord created me with an inquiring mind, and simplistic, pat answers never worked for me. Over the years, I began to discover that He actually enjoyed my questionings, and my seeking to know Him more intimately. The issues of pain, suffering, death, and grief were not simply academic subjects, but they were everyday experiences in the lives of people all around us. As pastors, Charles and I soon learned that there were broken hearts and lives in every pew of our churches, all seeking for comfort and answers. With an aching heart, I once again turned to searching the Scriptures for some answers. The Holy Spirit would be my Teacher.

> *However, when He, the Spirit of truth,*
> *has come, He will guide you into all truth;*
> *for He will not speak on His own authority,*
> *but whatever He hears He will speak; and He*
> *will tell you things to come. He will glorify Me,*
> *for He will take of what is Mine*
> *and declare it to you.*
> John 16:13,14

I had learned through the years that the Holy Spirit was not only my wonderful Counselor, but He was also the Teacher of truth and revelation. He would guide me to discover His truth. My first insights came from the study of the heroes of faith in Hebrews 11. The first 35 verses are exciting, inspiring, and just what you would expect to see happen for people living with faith in God. Then the word "others" jumped from the page, and caused me to carefully reread and ponder the following words:

*Women received their dead raised to life
again. Others were tortured, not accepting
deliverance, that they might obtain a
better resurrection. Still others had trial of
mockings and scourgings, yes, and of chains
and imprisonment. They were stoned, they
were sawn in two, were tempted, were slain
with the sword. They wandered about in
sheepskins and goatskins, being destitute,
afflicted, tormented—of whom the world was
not worthy. They wandered in deserts and
mountains, in dens and caves of the earth.*
Hebrews 11:35-38

Slowly, I reread the whole passage from different translations. It became very clear that both those who by faith saw such miraculous events happen, and those who suffered and died in faith "were all commended for their faith, yet none of them received what had been promised."

*And all these, having obtained
a good testimony through faith,
did not receive the promise. . . .*
Hebrews 11:39

My mind returned to verse 13, "All these people were still living by faith when they died!" Deep in my spirit, I kept hearing the phrase, "You need a greater eternal perspective, My daughter." My mind quickly went back to II Corinthians 4:17,18, and the words "eternal glory," "seen versus unseen," and "temporary versus eternal." The unseen spiritual world was the eternal reality of life. The

Lord has given us eternal promises and because of this eternal reality, God's promises can also find their completion and fulfillment in future generations. The more I studied, read and pondered, it soon became clear that all believing prayer offered in His will and in His name will be answered, but not always in our lifetime:

These all died in faith, not having received
the promises, but having seen them afar
off were assured of them, embraced them
and confessed that they were strangers and
pilgrims on the earth.
Hebrews 11:13

There is a striking example in the book of Acts of the often baffling and mysterious ways of God. We observe this in the life of Stephen in Acts 7. In fact, from a human perspective these events seem very illogical and quite a waste for the purposes of the kingdom. A "waste," that is, if you only have a limited, earthly perspective, and not an eternal perspective. The account of the stoning of Stephen is a riveting account of the brief life of a man who was chosen as a servant-leader to "wait on tables." To qualify for this job, he needed to be a man "full of the Spirit and wisdom." Acts 6:5 describes him as "a man full of faith and of the Holy Spirit." In Acts 6:8 Luke continues to describe this extraordinary deacon:

And Stephen, full of faith and power,
did great wonders and signs among the people.

It would certainly appear as if Stephen had a powerful destiny ahead of him in the establishment of the young,

84

fragile, 1ˢᵗ century church. Nevertheless, before long this anointed, faith-filled man of God, whose "face was like the face of an angel," would be stoned to death and taken from the earthly scene. How much sense does this make? Why would God allow this? From the content of Acts 7, it is obvious that Stephen had given himself to much study of the Scripture. His knowledge and presentation of the Gospel was masterful, anointed, and bold.

It is perhaps the account of Acts 7:54-8:1 that gives us some powerful and beautiful insights into the Lord's heart and ways:

> *When they heard these things they were cut to the heart, and they gnashed at him with their teeth. But he, being full of the Holy Spirit, gazed into heaven and saw the glory of God, and Jesus standing at the right hand of God, and said, "Look! I see the heavens opened and the Son of Man standing at the right hand of God!" Then they cried out with a loud voice, stopped their ears, and ran at him with one accord; and they cast him out of the city and stoned him. And the witnesses laid down their clothes at the feet of a young man named Saul. And they stoned Stephen as he was calling on God and saying, "Lord Jesus, receive my spirit." Then he knelt down and cried out with a loud voice, "Lord, do not charge them with this sin." And when he had said this, he fell asleep. Now Saul was consenting to his death. At that time a great persecution arose against the church which was at Jerusalem; and they were all*

*scattered throughout the regions of Judea and
Samaria, except the apostles.*

Many years ago, I remember Charles teaching from the book of Hebrews. Jesus, our High Priest, after He finished the profound work of salvation, sat down at the right hand of the Father. We observed that there were no chairs in the Old Testament tabernacle and temple. The priests could never sit down; their work of bringing sacrifice for the atonement of sin was never finished. But, when Jesus died as our High Priest, the work of salvation was completed and accomplished once and for all!

*But this Man, after He had offered
one sacrifice for sins forever, sat down
at the right hand of God. . . .*
Hebrews 10:12

With all my heart I worshipped Jesus for His finished work of salvation reflected in the statement: "He sat down." As we were praising Him, I heard these words whispered into my heart, "Except for one time." Immediately the events surrounding Stephen's death in Acts 7 came to my remembrance:

*But he, being full of the Holy Spirit, gazed into
heaven and saw the glory of God, and Jesus
standing at the right hand of God, and said,
"Look! I see the heavens opened and the Son of
Man standing at the right hand of God!"*
Acts 7:55,56

The Holy Spirit began to bring revelation to my seeking heart. "Lord, why are You, who are now *seated* at the right hand of the Father, standing for Your servant Stephen?" Immediately I received a picture of a huge football stadium filled to capacity with cheering crowds of people. As the home team scored a touchdown, every one of the fans was on their feet, cheering, applauding, and jumping!

Then I understood. Stephen had scored a touchdown for the Kingdom. He had allowed Jesus to so work in his life that he now reflected the very image and likeness of His Savior. Stephen's dying words sounded awesomely familiar in the portals of heaven: "Lord, do not hold this sin against them." No wonder Jesus stood. He could hardly wait to give His beloved friend a rich, joy-filled welcome into the eternal kingdom. I can almost see the smile on Jesus' face. Perhaps He said to all of heaven, "This is what I died for, to bring a whole host of sons and daughters conformed to My image, into My eternal kingdom."

Little did Stephen then know that his prayer for forgiveness would both torment, and finally triumph, in the life of one standing by, "giving approval to his death," Saul of Tarsus, who would soon become Paul, the apostle.

"Most assuredly, I say to you, unless a grain of wheat falls into the ground and dies, it remains alone; but if it dies, it produces much grain."
John 12:24

Did the Lord answer all of my questions concerning Betty and her seemingly premature death? No, not all, but He did give me a revelation into His heart that took me from questioning to quietly worshipping a God who would never cease to amaze and encourage me to continue to seek Him with all my heart.

Thank you, Lord, that when we cannot "trace Your hand, we can always trust Your heart." Increase our spiritual vision of eternal realities, and continue to unfold for us the beauty of Your heart and Your ways.

Precious Tears

You number my wanderings;
put my tears into Your bottle;
are they not in Your book?
Psalm 56:8

*I*t has been said that nearly all God's jewels are crystallized tears. C.H. Spurgeon wrote that tears are liquid prayers. The psalmist writes:

Those who sow in tears shall reap in joy. He
who continually goes forth weeping, bearing
seed for sowing, shall doubtless come again
with rejoicing, bringing his sheaves with him.
Psalm 126:5,6

Science suggests that tears have healing properties in them helping to release some of the toxic build up coming from the emotional pool of pain and stress that accompanies living life. There are tears of joy and tears of sadness and grief. Of the latter, John gives us a beautiful, comforting promise:

And God will wipe away every tear from their
eyes; there shall be no more death, nor sorrow,
nor crying. There shall be no more pain, for the
former things have passed away.
Revelation 21:4

From the study of tears in Scripture, I have concluded that the Lord is always moved by the overflow of tears from the hearts of His people. Tears speak when words cannot. Tears are a gift from the Lord.

One very touching account on the power of tears comes from the story of Mary Magdalene in John 20. She is one intriguing woman to study and from whom to learn. Her name first appears in Luke 8:2. Writing of those who traveled with Jesus, Luke speaks of the women.

. . .and certain women who had been
healed of evil spirits and infirmities—
Mary called Magdalene, out of whom had
come seven demons. . . .
Luke 8:2

"Out of her came seven demons." This statement is certainly an attention grabber! What does a woman look like, feel like, and act like, who is possessed by seven demons? How did she get that way, and how did she encounter Jesus? All of these questions are specifically left unanswered, but one thing we do know is that this broken, lost, driven woman one day met her Savior and was forever transformed. She who was an anguished, captive woman of the demonic world, through Jesus' love and deliverance became a free, vibrant woman fulfilling her God-given destiny.

Mary Magdalene's name appears repeatedly in the New Testament accounts of the crucifixion and burial of Jesus. While His disciples fled in fear, Mary stood with the other women in bewilderment and anguish at the unfolding of such horrific events. How could someone who had brought her such life and purpose be so brutally beaten and killed? She watched Him being laid in the tomb, and her painful confusion and broken-heartedness only increased. How could this be happening; why would it be happening? The women lingered as long as they could, but then had to reluctantly leave to observe the Sabbath, and do the only thing they knew to do – prepare spices and perfumes for the dead body of their beloved Master.

And then it happened! Very early, in the mist of pre-dawn, carrying all the spices and perfume they had worked so hard to prepare, they stood before a tomb much different from the one they had left. The stone was moved, and most shocking of all, it was empty, except for two angels sitting in the tomb that was now empty of Jesus' dead body. Imagine yourself being there. Try to feel what this stunned woman was experiencing. In her total state of shock and bewilderment, Mary is asked a question that would reverberate throughout the ages.

> *Jesus said to her, "Woman why are you*
> *weeping? Whom are you seeking?"*
> *She supposing Him to be the gardener,*
> *said to Him, "Sir, if you have carried Him away,*

tell me where you have laid Him,
and I will take Him away."
John 20:15

In the midst of our tears and losses in life, we are asked the same probing question, w*hy* are we crying? And w*ho* and *what* are we looking for in our most desperate hour?

How easily we forget the words of our Savior when our world feels like it's been turned upside down. How often He calls to us to remember His words and promises. Luke 24:5-8 begin with:

"Why do you seek the living among the dead?"
"He is not here, but risen! Remember how
He spoke to you when He was still in Galilee,
saying, 'The Son of Man must be delivered into
the hands of sinful men, and be crucified and
the third day rise again.'"

This powerful passage on how the risen Savior responded to Mary's tears at the tomb deeply moved, inspired, and encouraged me. As I read and reread the passage, I asked the Lord to bring illumination and revelation into my heart and mind. Always when studying and meditating in the Scripture, I'm reminded of an old hymn that states: "Beyond the sacred page I seek Your face, O Lord." Once again I had the joy of discovering a fresh nugget of truth about the wonder of the Lord we serve.

Just consider all of the people to whom Jesus could have first appeared. I sure would want to break down the doors of the religious Sanhedrin and say, "Aha, here

I am," or perhaps go to Pilate, or some other important people. Then it dawned on me, He had nothing to prove or defend. He had done it all, and victory was complete!

But to whom was He drawn? Who was the first person to whom He appeared in His resurrection? Jesus came first to a grieving, weeping woman!! Absolutely amazing! What drew Him to her? Other women had also anointed Him with tears of utter adoration and love, but here was Mary at the empty tomb, desperate for her Savior. And it is to her He revealed Himself, and to her also was given the great commission to tell others:

> *Jesus said to her, "Do not cling to Me, for I have not yet ascended to My Father; but go to My brethren and say to them, I am ascending to My Father and your Father, and to My God and your God."*
> John 20:17

Mary was entering a new season of intimate friendship with the Lord. In essence He told her that there was much more to knowing and loving Him than she had previously experienced.

So it is for us. We do not easily embrace change. The fact is that most of us move into the deeper places in God with tears and trepidation about the uncertainties of this new place. Mary was on a journey of new discoveries. For her to embrace them, she would have to adjust to a new and more intimate way of relating to Him. She would now live a life where Jesus was not only *with* her but would be *in* her. Mary had to also abandon even the good and thrilling days of her past way of relating to Him, and fully embrace the new, where she lived not by sight, but by a rich faith in her risen Lord. This new season required a greater availability to Him in both obedience and proclamation. Yes, Jesus does still turn our mourning into dancing, and our tears into treasure discovered in the secret place of His heart.

Then shall the virgin rejoice in the dance, and
the young men and the old, together; for I will
turn their mourning to joy, will comfort them,
and make them rejoice rather than sorrow.
Jeremiah 31:13

Thank You, Father, for always being there for us in our valley of tears, and for turning these valleys into springs of praise and blessings. Even in our grief and sorrows You are the treasure we seek. We thank You for every change that brings us closer to Yourself.

HOPE FOR THE HOPELESS

*Now may the God of hope fill you with all joy
and peace in believing, that you may abound in
hope by the power of the Holy Spirit.*
Romans 15:13

We live in a world often gripped by the feelings of hopelessness. Hopelessness often results from wrong choices we or others around us have made. The events happening around us over which we have no control can also come tumbling down around us. How do we live, endure, and maintain hope in spite of the suffering and pain around us? As the end-times continue to move in on us, despair, discouragement, and hopelessness will also increase, and the Christian is a main target for serious attacks from the enemy.

Often in life, I have felt so discouraged by circumstances around me that it was an effort to get out of bed and face the day. I remember sitting in my back yard wondering if we would ever see our way through these oppressive, discouraging happenings. I felt desperate for some encouraging hope-filled word. "O God, where are You?"

Thankfully, I had learned early in life to go to the Scriptures, regardless of how I felt or how hopeless I thought life was. It is important to make choices in the light that will help sustain and guide us when things become dark.

For whatever things were written before were written for our learning, that we through the patience and comfort of the Scriptures might have hope.
Romans 15:4

As I began to review what I objectively knew to be true about the Lord, both from diligent study and past personal encounter and experience, I realized that He seemed to specialize in what appeared to be hopeless situations. A favorite passage of mine from Mark 5:24-34 came to my discouraged heart:

So Jesus went with him, and a great multitude followed Him and thronged Him. Now a certain woman had a flow of blood for twelve years, and had suffered many things from many physicians. She had spent all that she had and was no better, but rather grew worse. When she heard about Jesus, she came behind Him in the crowd and touched His garment. For she said, "If only I may touch His clothes, I shall be made well." Immediately the fountain of her blood was dried up, and she felt in her body that she was healed of the affliction. And Jesus, immediately knowing in Himself that power had gone out of Him, turned around in the crowd and said, "Who touched My clothes?"

But His disciples said to Him, "You see the multitude thronging You, and You say, 'Who touched Me?'" And He looked around to see her who had done this thing. But the woman, fearing and trembling, knowing what had happened to her, came and fell down before Him and told Him the whole truth. And He said to her, "Daughter, your faith has made you well. Go in peace, and be healed of your affliction."

If ever there was a hopeless woman in a hopeless condition it was this woman. As always when I read these stories, I attempt to see them as if I were in the crowd. I try to imagine how this woman felt. What motivated her actions? Jesus was literally surrounded by so many people, that the crowds were pressing in on him, and a desperate, hopeless, despairing woman was there in the midst. This was a rather reckless thing for her to do, because her constant bleeding of 12 years made her ceremonially as "unclean" as any leper. In fact, the story reveals to us that she tried repeatedly to get help from many doctors, but only became worse. For 12 years she experienced the social stigma of being rejected by her family, culture, and even her religion. Homeless, sick, fatigued, and nowhere to go — what kept her going, I wondered, and what brought her there into the midst of this crowd?

Then I read these words: "When she heard about Jesus" (v. 27). I was arrested by these words. What did the woman hear? Who did she hear them from? Nothing is specifically given to answer these questions, but we can just imagine. Because she was a "social reject," I imagine her hanging out in the shadows, hiding, fearful, and yet so very desperate for some human voices. Then it happened! She heard a conversation about the man Jesus, who some called the Messiah. He healed the sick, opened blind eyes, raised the dead, forgave sins, and declared that He alone was the way, the truth, and the life for people. He offered Himself as the Bread of life for the hungry, the Light of the world for those in darkness, and declared He was the Good Shepherd for lost, mangled, and torn sheep. And for her personally, most startling, this Jesus touched and healed a leper, an outcast just like she was. While I considered this passage, I could almost feel the spark of hope that began to flicker in her heart. As the Holy Spirit was bringing hope and encouragement to me through these Scriptures, I heard Him ask: "And what seeds are planted in the hearts of people around you as they happen to overhear your conversations?" I was reminded that ". . .faith comes from hearing the message, and the message is heard through the Word of Christ" (Romans 10:17 NIV). There is power in testimony!

Whatever this woman heard, it worked faith in her heart, and she boldly, almost recklessly, did what was not only unusual, but what was also "forbidden" by the Levitical law for someone declared to be unclean. Faith arose within her from the ashes of disappointment and hopelessness, and she mustered up what little strength she had left to press through the crowd. She touched His cloak, touched just the hem of His garment, and "immediately her bleeding stopped and she felt in her body that she was freed from her suffering" (v 29). When I meet her in the eternal scene, there are just so many questions I want to ask her. What did it feel like to be free from bleeding after 12 long years? What did it feel like to be free of 12 years of suffering? Did others around her know who she was? What happened to her afterwards?

This precious story is not finished yet. Just imagine the woman getting swallowed up in the large crowd, and then Jesus stopped. He kept turning around asking, "Who touched Me?" Now how did she feel? Why would He expose her this way? But Jesus looked around to see who had done it. It is hard to imagine what this woman was thinking and feeling, but finally she inched forward, fell at His feet, and trembling with fear, "told Him the whole truth" (v. 33). She told Him the whole truth! Then even a greater miracle took place. In those next few minutes, it was only Jesus and her. At His feet I believe she poured out all of her anguish, shame, pain, discouragement, and hopelessness. This sad woman, orphaned from both family and society around her, continued to give Him her broken heart and shattered dreams. She told Him the whole truth, and in those next moments, not only was her body healed, but even more so was her shattered, hopeless heart healed and restored, as she heard words of life.

"Daughter, your faith has healed you. Go in
peace and be freed from your suffering." (v. 34)

Daughter! With this word He not only healed her heart, but He also publicly wiped away the years of shame and rejection. Here, in the midst of a large crowd, He publicly owned her as His daughter. He publicly once again restored her place, not only to her own family and friends, but He restored her to Himself as His own daughter.

As I read and reread these words of life, I began to thank Him that He always brings hope to the hopeless. While I reflected upon the many examples in Scripture, I soon realized that even when one loves and serves the Lord, there will be times of discouragement and almost hopelessness. It is in times like these that we must learn to encourage ourselves in the Lord even as David did in I Samuel 30, and as Paul did in II Timothy 4:16-18:

> *At my first defense no one stood with me,*
> *but all forsook me. May it not be charged*
> *against them. But the Lord stood with me and*
> *strengthened me, so that the message might*
> *be preached fully through me, and that all the*
> *Gentiles might hear. Also I was delivered out of*
> *the mouth of the lion. And the Lord will deliver*
> *me from every evil work and preserve me for*
> *His heavenly kingdom. To Him be glory forever*
> *and ever. Amen!*

Thank you, Jesus, that You are the God of hope. Thank you that You can always be depended upon to breathe into us the encouragement and the hope we do desperately need as we live in this increasingly dark world.

THE POWER OF JOY AND LAUGHTER

He will yet fill your mouth with laughing,
and your lips with rejoicing.
Job 8:21

Your testimonies I have taken as a heritage
forever, for they are the rejoicing of my heart.
Psalm 119:111

We live in a very broken and fractured world. The reality of evil and the relentless assaults of the world around us seem to make a mockery of the angels' declarations:

Then the angel said to them, "Do not be afraid,
for behold, I bring you good tidings of great joy
which will be to all people . . . Glory to God in
the highest, and on earth peace,
goodwill toward men!"
Luke 2:10,14

And yet deep within each of us is a yearning for abiding peace and overflowing joy. In fact, today science itself is speaking out on the benefits of joy and laughter to the mental, emotional, and physical well-being of every individual. The experience of joy and laughter in daily life greatly contributes to a person's well-being and productivity.

The Scriptures abound in admonitions to be ever-rejoicing and full of joy. Here are only a few to consider:

> *Make a joyful shout to the Lord, all you lands!*
> *Serve the Lord with gladness; come before His*
> *presence with singing.*
> Psalm 100:1,2

> *Oh come, let us sing to the Lord! Let us shout*
> *joyfully to the Rock of our salvation.*
> Psalm 95:1

> *A glad heart makes a cheerful countenance,*
> *but by sorrow of heart the spirit is broken.*
> Proverbs 15:13 AMP

> *A happy heart is good medicine and a cheerful*
> *mind works healing, but a broken spirit dries up*
> *the bones.*
> Proverbs 17:22 AMP

The Scriptures teach that joy is a gift:

> *"As the Father loved Me, I also have loved*
> *you; abide in My love. If you keep My*
> *commandments, you will abide in My love, just*
> *as I have kept My Father's commandments and*

abide in His love. These things I have spoken to you, that My joy may remain in you, and that your joy may be full."
John 15:9-11

Joy is a fruit of the Spirit cultivated in our lives through daily experiences of trials, testings, and choices we make.

But the fruit of the Spirit is love, joy, peace, longsuffering, kindness, goodness, faithfulness. . . .
Galatians 5:22

Joy is also a choice. In the book of Acts, Luke described what happened to Paul and Silas while they were preaching in Phillippi.

Then the multitude rose up together against them; and the magistrates tore off their clothes and commanded them to be beaten with rods. And when they had laid many stripes on them, they threw them into prison, commanding the jailer to keep them securely. Having received such a charge, he put them into the inner prison and fastened their feet in the stocks. But at midnight Paul and Silas were praying and singing hymns to God, and the prisoners were listening to them. Suddenly there was a great earthquake, so that the foundations of the prison were shaken; and immediately all the doors were opened and everyone's chains were loosed. And the keeper of the prison, awaking from sleep and seeing the prison doors open,

supposing the prisoners had fled, drew his sword and was about to kill himself. But Paul called with a loud voice, saying, "Do yourself no harm, for we are all here." Then he called for a light, ran in, and fell down trembling before Paul and Silas. And he brought them out and said, "Sirs, what must I do to be saved?" So they said, "Believe on the Lord Jesus Christ, and you will be saved, you and your household." Then they spoke the word of the Lord to him and to all who were in his house. And he took them the same hour of the night and washed their stripes. And immediately he and all his family were baptized. Now when he had brought them into his house, he set food before them; and he rejoiced, having believed in God with all his household.
Acts 16: 22-34

We can also imagine the scene in Acts 14:19:

Then Jews from Antioch and Iconium came there; and having persuaded the multitudes, they stoned Paul and dragged him out of the city, supposing him to be dead.

Imagine the scene. Paul was stoned, and apparently so badly torn up in his body that they left him for dead. Most scholars believe that it was in this desperate place of impending physical death that he was taken into the third heaven, into paradise (II Corinthians 12:1-4). There Paul saw and heard things that he could find no earthly words to describe. As I have pondered and meditated on these Scriptures, I have a "holy hunch." From the rest of Paul's writings, I sense that what he saw and heard was such a profound revelation into the majesty of who Jesus is, and of what He has accomplished through His death on the cross, that these truths flowed like a powerful river of revelation in everything Paul wrote.

Herein is a key to entering into the "fellowship of His sufferings." As we hide ourselves in Him, in the secret place, He shares with us secrets of His heart that bring to us some of the greatest joys of life. David discovered this truth through the experiences of his own, at times very turbulent and sorrowful life:

> *The secret of the Lord is with those who fear*
> *Him, and He will show them His covenant.*
> Psalm 25:14

> *Whom have I in heaven but You? And there is*
> *none upon earth that I desire besides You. My*
> *flesh and my heart fail; but God is the strength*
> *of my heart and my portion forever.*
> Psalm 73:25,26

From the study of Scripture, we discover that nourishing thoughts, wholesome and positive patterns of thinking, are essential to living a rich life of joy and productivity. Joy also flows as a result of meaningful relationships. The most powerful experience of joy comes from a relationship with the God who knows everything about me and who still loves and enjoys my friendship. The overflow of this joy-filled relationship with God is to meaningfully connect and relate to those around me. Life becomes rich with meaning and purpose when we are in relationship with those we love and who love us and are genuinely glad to be with us. One of the questions I enjoy asking my family and friends is if I am fun to live and be with. (My daughters love to respond with: "Well, most of the time, Mom.")

Upon studying the subject of joy and laughter, both in Scripture and in secular resources, I have concluded that we as believers in Jesus owe it to the world to be super-naturally and extravagantly full of joy and peace. By God's grace we especially owe it to our families and our friends to cultivate around us an atmosphere of gratitude, joy, and laughter. It is important to realize that this kind of joy and laughter must be cultivated, not because the circumstances are always conducive to joy, but most often in spite of negative happenings. These end-times are requiring a people who receive joy as a gift from Jesus, who yield to the Holy Spirit's dealing in order to produce the fruit of joy, and who consistently learn to choose to rejoice regardless of circumstances.

Recently as I was pondering the very sad and traumatic events of Jesus' experience in Gethsemane, I was sobered by the fact that all of Jesus' disciples fell asleep when He needed them the most. It is only Luke who gives us some understanding as to why the disciples fell asleep.

When He rose up from prayer,
and had come to His disciples,
He found them sleeping from sorrow.
Luke 22:45

As I sat before the Lord, I began to discuss with Him the statement that the disciples fell asleep, ". . .exhausted from sorrow." Yes, the emotion of sorrow often causes one to become so exhausted that sleep seems to be the only place of relief.

"But Lord, what will keep Your end-time church awake during the increasing onslaughts of evil, grief, sadness, and calamities? What will keep us from falling asleep exhausted from the sorrows of these last days?" As I quietly sat in His Presence, I clearly heard, "My end-time Bride will be baptized with a double portion of joy and laughter." Joy and laughter are some of the most powerful weapons of spiritual warfare in these last days. As we laugh and rejoice, the spirit of depression and despair will be broken. God's people will know that the joy of the Lord is their strength. May we each receive this precious baptism of His love, peace, and joy!

Now to Him who is able to keep you from stumbling, and to present you faultless before the presence of His glory with exceeding joy, to God our Savior, who alone is wise, be glory and majesty, dominion and power both now and forever. Amen.
Jude 24,25

Thank you, Jesus, for Your gift of joy. Thank you for the joy of our salvation, and for the joy of rich fellowship with You and Your people. Thank you, Lord, for teaching us that even in the darkest valleys, even with our hearts broken, we can lift our tear-stained faces to You and receive not only Your comfort, but also a deep baptism of Your love and joy which "passes all of our understanding." Thank you, Lord, for Peter's declaration at the end of his journey:

> *Though now you do not see Him,*
> *yet believing, you rejoice with joy*
> *inexpressible and full of glory. . . .*
> 1 Peter 1:8

THE WOUND OF DISAPPOINTMENT

Great peace have they who love your law,
nothing shall offend them
or make them stumble."
Psalm 119:165 AMP

*T*here are seasons in our journey with God that feel like we are walking through a bleak and barren desert. The press of circumstances and the relentless attacks of the enemy wear us out. We experience the joy-robbing emotions of deep disappointment, disillusion-ment, depression, discouragement, and often despair. These are only some of the deadly darts of the enemy through which he attempts to wound and defeat us. In the words of Joel 2:12b:

Surely the joy of mankind is withered away.

Withering joy may result from unconfessed sin and dis-obedience as well as from unhealed wounds of the soul. There is an adversary who is determined to destroy our dreams, and to rob us of our visions and hopes. But even though Satan attempts to take: ". . .joy and gladness from the house of God." (Joel 1: 16b), our God is determined to send us grain, new wine, and oil – all word pictures of the Holy Spirit. (Joel 2:19)

How vividly I am able to recall the dreams and visions that burned in us as teenagers. Our hearts were filled with excitement for the future. We were radically passionate for God, and then life happened. Even though I continued to serve Him in different ways, it sure didn't feel like we were changing the world. In fact, it didn't take long before deep disappointments in myself, in others, and even in God began to rob me of peace, joy, and energy. Life seemed at times to settle into a boring routine. Oh yes, we were serving the Lord, but something was missing! Then we found ourselves in the middle of the "Jesus People Movement," and the normal routines of life were drastically changed by the demands and needs of all those young people. And serve them we did! But in the middle of those wonderful days, something within me still felt empty.

One morning I realized I was too sick and exhausted to even get out of bed. As others took over my responsibilities, I simply stayed in bed feeling very discouraged. Why couldn't I get a break-through physically? I believed in healing, I confessed being healed for years, and still there I was. As the tears quietly fell, I heard His voice deep within my heart. "My child you are disappointed in Me." I immediately denied that this ungodly attitude could be in my heart. Then the Scripture, "Blessed is he who is not offended in Me," pierced my heart. I didn't even know where this Scripture was found or to whom it was said. Finally, as the Holy Spirit began brooding over my heart, I confessed that yes, there was an offense and a deep dis-appointment in my heart toward the Lord. I felt as if He had let me down! His promises didn't seem to be working for me. Why couldn't I get the promised break-through? Wasn't I trying to live and serve Him? This offense and dis-appointment caused my joy and energy to wither away.

Through the aid of a concordance I discovered that this word on offense was spoken to one who was among the most uniquely chosen of the Lord – John the Baptist. The account in Luke 7:18-23 is riveting and most thought provoking.

> *The disciples of John reported to him concerning all these things. And John, calling two of his disciples to him, sent them to Jesus, saying, "Are You the Coming One, or do we look for another?" When the men had come to Him, they said, "John the Baptist has sent us to You, saying, 'Are You the Coming One, or do we look for another?'" And that very hour He cured many of infirmities, afflictions and evil spirits; and to many blind He gave sight. Jesus answered and said to them, "Go and tell John the things you have seen and heard: that the blind see, the lame walk, the lepers are cleansed, the deaf hear, the dead are raised, the poor have the gospel preached to them. And blessed is he who is not offended because of Me."*

How could someone like John be brought to such a place of doubt and confusion? What happened to him? I thought about how he, who was so accustomed to living out in the wilderness, was now thrust into a dark, filthy, vermin infested, confining prison. As John remained in prison month after month, he heard of all the marvelous works of healings and miracles Jesus performed. Most likely the enemy was quick to whisper in his ear: "See, He does it for everyone else, but He has obviously forgotten you." When John's disciples told him of all these miracles, John sent them to ask Jesus: "Are you the one who was to come, or should we expect someone else?" How shocking a question is this coming from John the Baptist. It is important to see how Jesus answered his doubts. "The blind receive sight, the lame walk, those who have leprosy are cured, the deaf hear, the dead are raised and the good news is preached to the poor." As I pondered these words, I said, "Lord, these words would feel like salt being poured into a wound. If I were John, I would wonder why I was still suffering in a prison cell, when He who raised the dead could easily get me out." But then Jesus concluded His response to John with this most powerful statement:

> *"And blessed (happy – with life – joy and*
> *satisfaction in God's favor and salvation, apart*
> *from outward conditions – and to be envied)*
> *is he who takes no offense in Me and who is*
> *not hurt or resentful or annoyed or repelled or*
> *made to stumble [whatever may occur]."*
> Luke 7:23 AMP

This Word both pierced and began a healing in my disappointed and doubting heart. Deep within I heard the illuminating voice of my beloved Shepherd. "My daughter I call you to trust Me, especially when you feel you are in a dark prison of circumstances. Even when it appears that I am answering the cries and prayer of others, will you still trust Me? Will you praise Me, even in your darkness and confusion, and will you refuse to take offense no matter what I do or don't do?"

I lay there on my bed quietly weeping as once again His Word performed a strategic surgical and healing incision into the secret places of my soul. His goodness brought me to repentance and a place of freedom. Indeed, hadn't Job himself come to this place?

"Though He slay me, yet will I trust Him."
Job 13:15a

My life was changed that morning. My Lord restored to me the joy of my salvation. As He washed me of my disappointments and disillusionments, I experienced a new freedom of joy, health, and communion with Him. The good Shepherd had once again restored my soul, something He would do repeatedly in my journey with Him into the secret places.

Father, thank You for the power of Your Word. Thank You that You desire truth in the "inward parts" and that Your Holy Spirit loves to bring healing conviction and repentance to our hearts. And thank You that when "we can't trace Your hand we can always trust Your heart." You are our rich treasure!

FIGHTING MAD

But the wisdom that is from above is first pure,
then peaceable, gentle, willing to yield, full
of mercy and good fruits, without partiality
and without hypocrisy. Now the fruit of
righteousness is sown in peace by those who
make peace.
James 3:17,18

I slammed the bedroom door, and just stood in the middle of the room trying to calm myself down. It was not fair! Just who did they think they were!

It was the early 70's. We were in the midst of the Jesus Movement, and our home was literally filled with young people who had just found the Lord. A number of them actually moved in with us. As the months progressed, some of these young people came across a teaching on women being silent in the church. They began to share their opinions and materials on the subject, and even though Charles did not agree with this view of Scripture, the atmosphere during our gathering times became quite oppressive for the women.

When I was told that some of them would no longer listen to any of us women share publicly, I became hurt and very angry. After all, I had been sharing from the Scriptures for longer than most of them had been living. To study and to share with others the Word of God was one of my greatest joys in life. And now, this was no longer permissible! To say I was "fighting mad" was an understatement! As the months progressed, my feelings of hurt turned into anger, and anger was now slowly becoming a root of bitterness growing within me.

As this was happening, communion with the Lord was also slipping away to a rote routine. But early in my life, the Lord had "ruined" me! He had given me such a life-changing encounter with Himself that I literally experienced a "blessed ruination" – nothing and no one could ever again satisfy my deepest longings; only Jesus would truly satisfy the longings of my heart.

I remember dragging myself into Charles' small study, plopping down on the chair, and with tears freely flowing, confessing, "Lord, I'm lonely for You." I wept in repentance, confessing my angry and defensive attitudes. I still remember telling Him that even if I never again publicly shared from His Word, the gift and calling was His and not mine, I would trust Him. Much more transpired in that little study that afternoon, some of which was for Him and me alone to know and remember, but soon His Presence washed over me, and once again the voice of my Shepherd spoke:

"My daughter, you have your mouth defensively open so much I can't get in one word." Then into my mind came this powerful Scripture:

> *. . .who, when He was reviled,*
> *did not revile in return; when He suffered,*
> *He did not threaten, but committed Himself to*
> *Him who judges righteously. . . .*
> I Peter 2:23

As I meditated on Jesus' example, another Scripture came to mind which would forever change my life and understanding of His awesome ways and of His heart. The account is found in Mark 14:3-9:

> *And being in Bethany at the house of Simon the*
> *leper, as He sat at the table, a woman came*
> *having an alabaster flask of very costly oil of*
> *spikenard. Then she broke the flask and poured*
> *it on His head. But there were some who were*
> *indignant among themselves, and said, "Why*
> *was this fragrant oil wasted? For it might have*
> *been sold for more than three hundred denarii*
> *and given to the poor." And they criticized her*
> *sharply. But Jesus said, "Let her alone. Why do*
> *you trouble her? She has done a good work for*
> *Me. For you have the poor with you always,*
> *and whenever you wish you may do them*
> *good; but Me you do not have always. She has*
> *done what she could. She has come beforehand*
> *to anoint My body for burial. Assuredly, I say*
> *to you, wherever this gospel is preached in the*

*whole world, what this woman has done will
also be told as a memorial to her."*

This was precious Mary of Bethany, who had sat listening to the words and heart of Jesus.

*Now it happened as they went that He entered
a certain village; and a certain woman named
Martha welcomed Him into her house. And
she had a sister called Mary, who also sat at
Jesus' feet and heard His word. But Martha
was distracted with much serving, and she
approached Him and said, "Lord, do You not
care that my sister has left me to serve alone?
Therefore tell her to help me." And Jesus
answered and said to her, "Martha, Martha,
you are worried and troubled about many
things. But one thing is needed, and Mary has
chosen that good part, which will not be taken
away from her."*
Luke 10:38-42

This was Mary, whose faith hit a brick wall of confusion, heartache, and disappointment. In spite of their desperate pleas to Jesus for help and intervention, Mary watched her brother, Lazarus, die (John 11). This same Mary, who had walked through her own difficult journey of "the valley of the shadow of death," obviously had discovered a deeper revelation of her Savior's heart. It seems as if she alone really understood what was before her beloved Lord.

As I read and reread this beautiful passage, I heard the Holy Spirit ask me some questions. "When Mary broke the alabaster jar, how did the disciples respond? As I reread the passage, the words, "And they rebuked her harshly," jumped off the page. The disciples were angry and very strongly condemned her wasteful extravagance (especially Judas). I then heard Him ask: "And how did Mary respond to their harsh rebuke?" I read and reread, and finally with a flash of insight said, "Why Lord, she didn't say a word in her defense." It then dawned on me that Mary was so involved in loving worship and ministry to Jesus, that she probably didn't even hear them! Then, as if with a smile on His face, I heard: "And who spoke on her behalf?" With tears of joyful discovery running down my face, I realized that it was Jesus Himself who came to her defense!

There were three words found in the NIV translation that flooded my heart with illumination. Mary *broke* the jar and poured it on Him (Mark 14:3), Jesus said she had done a *beautiful* thing to Him (v. 6), and Mary did this act of worship *beforehand* to prepare for His burial (v. 8). My mind was definitely being renewed and transformed through the revelation of His Word.

> *And do not be conformed to this world, but*
> *be transformed by the renewing of your mind,*
> *that you may prove what is that good and*
> *acceptable and perfect will of God.*
> Romans 12:2

It is only through brokenness and humility that true worship is poured out upon Jesus. This expression of

loving worship ministers something beautiful to Him,
and is something He treasures and cherishes. Mary did
a very profoundly beautiful pouring out of love and worship beforehand. A day will shortly be here when every
knee will bow, and every tongue confess that Jesus Christ
is Lord, to the glory of the Father:

> *. . .that at the name of Jesus every knee should
> bow, of those in heaven, and of those on earth,
> and of those under the earth, and that every
> tongue should confess that Jesus Christ is Lord,
> to the glory of God the Father.*
> Philippians 2:10,11

But we who are the redeemed of the Lord, we who
have received Him in this the day of salvation, are privileged to bow our knees in joyful adoration, and to worship freely and willingly, and to do it *beforehand!*

I left that small study changed by His rhema Word to
my heart and mind. His living Word once again brought
amazing peace and joy. Very little changed in our gatherings, but my heart was free to worship and adore Him. No
matter what else was happening, we were all free to sing
and shout, "Worthy is the Lamb."

Then it happened! We were visited for the first time by
a highly respected older prophet of the Lord, C. L. Moore.
He was often referred to as the laughing prophet who
prophesied in rhyme. I came into the gathering a little late,
and took a seat in the back of the room. In the middle of
his sharing, Brother Moore stopped, and looked straight
at me. He was silent for a moment and then started

laughing as he walked towards me. I felt both frightened and excited. He placed his hands upon my head and declared: "And no longer shalt thou be silent in the House of the Lord, for He Himself hath put a Word in thy mouth, and thou shalt clearly speak it." There were other very pertinent things he spoke which were for that hour and that time, but these words will always be clearly etched in my mind. I humbly and gratefully wept, along with some of the other sisters. A whole new atmosphere of freedom, and forgiveness washed through our gathering, and a deep healing of reconciliation took place in many of our hearts. Personally, I learned that to be "fighting mad" was very self-defeating, and dishonoring to the Lord, but to have a broken and contrite heart of loving worship to Him is to discover more profound treasure in the secret places of His heart. How very blessed we are to offer Him something beautiful through our brokenness and to worship Him beforehand. Soon all the earth will cry "Worthy is the Lamb," and we have the privilege of doing it now in the day of salvation.

Father, Your ways are beautiful. Thank You for Your patience with us, and for Your brooding over us to take us both higher and deeper into Your heart. And thank You, dearest Lord, that we can trust You to judge every situation in our lives fairly and justly. You are the joy and delight of our hearts.

THE SURPRISING FEAR OF THE LORD

He will be the sure foundation for your times,
a rich store of salvation and wisdom
and knowledge; the fear of the Lord is
the key to this treasure.
Isaiah 33:6 NIV

*T*he longer I walk with the Lord, the more I grow to love Him, and the more I am surprised by His unpredictable ways and methods of winning the hearts of men and women to Himself. For as long as I can remember, there has been a hunger and an intense quest arising from deep within me to penetrate into the awesome secrets of His heart and of His ways. From the writings of David in the Psalms we catch glimpses of a man who himself intensely pursued the Lord. David yearned to intimately know Him and to more clearly understand the secrets of His heart! Listen to the cries of David's yearnings:

As the deer pants for streams of water, so my
soul pants for you, O God. My soul thirsts for

*God, the living God. When can I go and meet
with God?*
Psalm 42:1,2 NIV

*O God, You are my God,
earnestly I seek you; my soul thirsts for you,
my body longs for you, in a dry and weary land
where there is no water.*
Psalm 63:1 NIV

*The secret [of the sweet, satisfying
companionship] of the Lord have they who
fear (revere and worship) Him, and He will
show them His covenant and reveal to them its
[deep, inner] meaning.*
Psalm 25:14 AMP

The Lord put a key into the hand of David which enabled him to open the heavens so that he could behold the very beauty and majesty of the God he loved so much. The "fear of the Lord" encompasses so very much of kingdom life. This "fear of the Lord" has nothing to do with the negative and destructive emotion of fear that often immobilizes us. Indeed Jesus died to deliver us from these irrational fears and anxieties.

The Scriptures are clear that we are redeemed from the fears that come from our fallen, unredeemed natures:

*For God has not given us the spirit of fear; but
of power, and of love, and of a sound mind.*
II Timothy 1:7

> *There is no fear in love.*
> *But perfect love drives out fear because fear*
> *has to do with punishment. The one who fears*
> *is not made perfect in love.*
> I John 4:18 NIV

Through Jesus' death on the cross we are especially delivered from the fear of death. As a young, inexperienced Mom, I could easily be brought to a place of fear and anxiety whenever my children became ill. Once while Charles and I were ministering in Nebraska, Dianna became ill. In an unfamiliar home, I walked the floors with her all night. The next day I felt far removed from the advertised "woman of God, conference Bible teacher." In fact, I was so tired and anxious about Dianna, I couldn't even imagine myself teaching that morning. The hostess of the home took one look at me, and told me to sit down so she could pray over me and Dianna. As she prayed, she paused and said she sensed that I was bound by a fear of death. She then quoted Hebrews 2:14,15 (NIV):

> *Since the children have flesh and blood,*
> *he too shared in their humanity so that by his*
> *death he might destroy him who holds the*
> *power of death – that is, the devil – and free*
> *those who all their lives were held in slavery by*
> *their fear of death.*

Once again the entrance of His Word brought light, revelation, and deliverance to my soul. His perfect love does drive out all ungodly fear, and we are then free to discover the transforming, healing power of the Biblical fear of the Lord.

When we read the frequently used biblical phrase "the fear of the Lord," we know that there is a knowing of God that evokes from our deepest being a sense of awe, respect, honor, and worship of Him. Loving obedience comes from a living encounter with our majestically holy, loving, and omnipotent God. No wonder the writer of Proverbs states:

The fear of the LORD is the beginning
of wisdom, and the knowledge of
the Holy One is understanding.
Proverbs 9:10 NIV

The more David followed the passion of his heart to seek the Lord, the more he discovered that captivating beauty of the Lord in worship. As he worshipped, the revelation of His covenant and the purifying experience of the fear of the Lord was worked deeply into his soul.

The fear of the Lord is pure,
enduring forever. . . .
Psalm 19:9 NIV

As our knowledge of the Lord grows, so will a healthy, cleansing, and healing "fear of the Lord" increase. To know Him is to love Him, and to love Him is to obey Him. As His covenant is inscribed more deeply into the very fabric of our being, we become increasingly sensitive to that which either welcomes or grieves His Spirit. Proverbs 8:13 (NIV) clearly states:

To fear the Lord is to hate evil; I hate pride and
arrogance, evil behavior and perverse speech.

Because the intense cries for greater intimacy with Jesus, are now increasing from His Bride, He is answering with a fresh baptism of the Spirit and of fire. His Spirit brings life, and His fire brings holiness, and "the fear of the Lord."

As we pursue Him with all of our hearts, He will wonderfully surprise us with an awesome impartation of "the fear of the Lord" and the joy of discovering a vital key to the treasures of His heart.

> *Then those who feared the LORD talked with*
> *each other, and the LORD listened and heard.*
> *A scroll of remembrance was written in His*
> *presence concerning those who feared the*
> *LORD and honored His name.*
> Malachi 3:16 NIV

> *"But to you who fear My name, the Sun of*
> *Righteousness shall arise with healing in His*
> *wings; and you shall go out and grow fat like*
> *stall-fed calves."*
> Malachi 4:2

> *Come, you children, listen to me; I will teach*
> *you the fear of the LORD.*
> Psalm 34:11

Father, teach us the fear of the Lord in the way we think, the way we speak, and in the way we live our everyday lives, and open to us the treasures of Your heart.

We receive this Your promise, and celebrate its truth:

In the fear of the LORD there is strong
confidence, and His children will have a place
of refuge. The fear of the LORD is a fountain of
life, to turn one away from the snares of death.
Proverbs 14:26,27

WHAT WILL YOU DO WITH ME?

Do not labor for the food which perishes, but
for the food which endures to everlasting life,
which the Son of Man will give you, because
God the Father has set His seal on Him.
John 6:27

*T*he sanctuary was filled with praise and spontaneous cries for more of the Presence of the Lord. As we together called out to Him to come to us in revival power, I repeatedly cried out, "We welcome You, we welcome Your Presence in this house. Welcome, welcome Holy Spirit!" In the midst of our corporate cries of welcome, I heard His voice: "And what will you do with Me when I come?" Immediately the word from Luke 10:38-42 came into my heart and mind with a fresh, revelatory clarity:

Now it happened as they went that He entered
a certain village; and a certain woman named
Martha welcomed Him into her house. And
she had a sister called Mary, who also sat at
Jesus' feet and heard His word. But Martha
was distracted with much serving, and she

approached Him and said, "Lord, do You not care that my sister has left me to serve alone? Therefore tell her to help me." And Jesus answered and said to her, "Martha, Martha, you are worried and troubled about many things. But one thing is needed, and Mary has chosen that good part, which will not be taken away from her."

Imagine how excited and full of expectation the home of Martha, Mary, and Lazarus was. Jesus was coming, the one they loved, and who they knew deeply loved them. Luke told us that Martha welcomed Him and opened her home to Him. Everything had to be just right; only the best for her Master. Martha probably spent days planning and preparing for His coming. Most likely she thought of all the ways she could serve Him and make Him comfortable in their home. But what did Martha do after she welcomed Him? She became ". . .distracted by all the preparations that had to be made." How much like Martha we all are. We are frequently more concerned with doing than with being. Often we assume we know both what He needs and what He wants when we welcome Him into our lives, homes, and places of worship.

Martha assumed providing physical food would best serve her Master. As these verses unfold, we discover that Jesus had a deeper need than physical food. The storm of adversity and resistance was swirling around Him, and Jesus would be dead in about six months. He found that the religious order in Jerusalem, only about two miles from this wonderful, welcoming home in Bethany, wanted only to argue and debate and not to listen and learn!

The passage vividly unfolds for us both Jesus' need and His longing, and this is what dear, sensitive Mary gave to Him; she ". . .sat at the Lord's feet listening to what He said." She found a place of rest and quiet at His feet where she became focused to hear His every word. I wonder what she heard, what was being imparted to her as she sat at His feet listening? One thing we do know is that Jesus commended her choice: "Mary has chosen what is better, and it will not be taken from her." Mary chose to listen and to receive the words of life and truth coming from the lips of her Master. And in listening, His words became part of her life, not only then but for all eternity.

What about dear, beloved Martha? What did she do after she welcomed Him to her home? She became intensely busy serving Him. Some interesting things began to happen within Martha as her busy pace increased in the kitchen. She became increasingly critical, distracted, anxious, and pulled in many different directions. There was so much to do in serving Him, but where was her sister? As usual just sitting around. Martha's distracted heart and mind now became a battle-ground for the enemy's lies and distortions. Just imagine the accusing thoughts being directed toward Mary. Feelings of self pity also soon surfaced within Martha. Then most amazingly, her thoughts turned in accusation toward her beloved Lord! He, whom she just had so expectantly welcomed to her home, now became the object of her sharp accusation: "Lord, don't you care that my sister has left me to do the work by myself? Tell her to help me!" Wow, what a scathing rebuke against both Mary and Jesus coming out of Martha's mouth, and all of this in the midst of being so busy trying to serve Him!

When we become so distracted in serving, our capacity to hear our Lord's voice becomes dull, and vain imaginations often take over. Did Martha actually believe that Jesus didn't care? Jesus lovingly diagnosed Martha's real problem: "Martha . . . only one thing is needed."

Was Jesus suggesting Martha stop serving — never! However, He was emphasizing the need to hear His voice in the midst of serving. As great as Martha's food would taste, Jesus would have preferred a "crock-pot" dinner, simply cooking on the side. He was famished not for physical food, but for the nourishment He would receive from those who would listen and absorb His words into their very being. He longed to be believed in and to be listened to.

This lesson of busily serving and restfully sitting was most dramatically unfolded in my own life many years ago. One summer I found myself unexpectedly cooking for over 400 people at Camp Dominion in Northern Minnesota. Not only was I cooking, but I was also training the youth counselors, and leading the women's ministry. My day began at 5:00 A.M. and ended about midnight. It was during those intensely wonderful and exhausting days that Jesus again spoke to me from the passage on Martha and Mary. I could feel myself getting worried and upset about so many things when I heard Him say, "May I cook with you?" Amazing words of life! That summer I learned to cook with the Lord, and to commune with Him even as we were cooking, baking, peeling, and developing new and original Camp Dominion dishes. That summer was one of joy and laughter even in the midst of busy and intense activity. I realized that Jesus was not telling

Martha to stop serving, but He was refocusing her service to have its source in hearing His voice and listening to His words. "Speak, Lord, Your servant is listening," even in the midst of the busyness of life.

Father, we welcome You into our lives, our marriages, our work places, and our churches. We joyfully welcome You to speak into the deepest places of our hearts. To hear You speak the words of life is what our life is really about. Not only do we welcome You, we deeply love Your abiding, manifest Presence.

OUR DESTINY OF JOY AND HOPE

"For I know the thoughts that I think toward
you, says the LORD, thoughts of peace and not
of evil, to give you a future and a hope. Then
you will call upon Me and go and pray to Me,
and I will listen to you."
Jeremiah 29:1,12

*T*he beautiful jewels of joy and hope are some of the
richest discoveries I unearthed as treasure in some
of the darkest places of my life.

"I will give you the treasures of darkness and
hidden riches of secret places, that you may
know that I, the LORD, who call you by your
name, am the God of Israel."
Isaiah 45:3

It felt as if my heart and soul were being torn asunder
by the events swirling around us. Confusion, anger, dis-
rupted relationships, and painful accusations seemed to
be sucking the life out of me. "My God, where are You?"
was a constant cry erupting from the depths of my soul.

I especially remember one afternoon. It will always be etched in the memory bank of my mind. I was awaiting a letter from someone whom I loved and knew to be a friend. The house was empty of people when the mailman came. I ran to get the long awaited letter, went quickly into the house and expectantly tore it open. As I read its contents, it felt as if a knife pierced deeply into my heart, and worst of all, the God of my very life seemed to remain strangely silent. How deeply I entered into the piercing cry coming from David's heart:

> *"My God, My God, why have You forsaken Me?*
> *Why are You so far from helping Me, and from*
> *the words of My groaning? O My God, I cry in*
> *the daytime, but You do not hear; and in the*
> *night season, and am not silent."*
> Psalm 22:1,2

Then it happened! It was Thanksgiving weekend, and we were scheduled to spend the holidays in New York City with our family. As we drove along the New Jersey Turnpike in our little blue car, with all five of us plus the dog, we quickly filled the car with noise and chatter. Soon Charles called for a half hour of complete silence. As we zoomed past Exit 3, God's Presence suddenly and unexpectedly encompassed me. "I will now answer your cry, My daughter." There in the midst of our small crowded car, my beloved Lord took me into the secret place of His heart.

A passage of Scripture was clearly illuminated to my mind. I reached for the small New Testament that I always carried, and turned to Mark 14. This passage entered my heart and mind with refreshing and liberating insight.

Then they came to a place which was named
Gethsemane; and He said to His disciples,
"Sit here while I pray." And He took Peter,
James, and John with Him, and He began to be
troubled and deeply distressed. Then He said to
them, "My soul is exceedingly sorrowful, even
to death. Stay here and watch." He went a little
farther, and fell on the ground, and prayed that
if it were possible, the hour might pass from
Him. And He said, "Abba, Father, all things are
possible for You. Take this cup away from Me;
nevertheless, not what I will, but what You
will." Then He came and found them sleeping,
and said to Peter, "Simon, are you sleeping?
Could you not watch one hour? Watch and
pray, lest you enter into temptation. The spirit
indeed is willing, but the flesh is weak."
Mark 14:32-38

Visualize with me the traumatic events of that night. When Jesus was in Gethsemane, He entered into the very conflict of the ages. He wrestled with the very power of darkness for the salvation and redemption of the souls of mankind. In the midst of this struggle, His humanity cried out to His Father for help. He exclaimed that His sorrow was killing Him (v. 34). Looking to His disciples for some encouragement and solace, He found none, and as He stumbled back into the Presence of His Father, He loudly cried out:

"Daddy, Father, everything is possible for You.
Take this cup from me. Yet not what I will, but
what you will."
Mark 14:36

As I read and reread this passage, the Holy Spirit spoke clearly into my heart, "How, My daughter, do you think My heart felt when My beloved and cherished Son cried out to Me?" As I quietly communed with Him around this question, I asked: "Oh, my God, how did You stand it, how could You be silent to His cries?" In that very instant I heard a transforming word: "Because I knew the end of the matter!" Immediately, Hebrews 12:2 came to mind:

. . .looking unto Jesus, the author and finisher
of our faith, who for the joy that was set before
Him endured the cross, despising the shame,
and has sat down at the right hand of the
throne of God.

Jesus endured the shame, scorn, and deep pain, and humiliation of the cross because He too knew the end of the matter. He saw what His pain and death on the cross would actually accomplish. He looked down through the ages and saw the redemption of all of heaven and earth. He looked and saw you and me redeemed and restored to an intimacy of relationship with Himself.

As His Spirit continued to bring revelation and deeper understanding of His ways to my heart, I heard the quiet whisper of my good Shepherd: "And even so, My daughter, I see the end of the matter in your own life. Allow the pain of these days to press you closer to My heart, and I will bring you out into a wide place of joy, hope, and fruitful-ness."

And today, many years later, I find myself smiling in His Presence. Learning to not waste any of the griefs and sorrows of this life by mumbling, complaining, foolish speaking, and unbelief, has been treasure gleaned in the secret place of His heart and of His Word. Diligently medi-tating in His Word, and letting it shape my thinking and attitudes has released from deep within me a rich river of joy and hope.

For I consider that the sufferings of this present time are not worthy to be compared with the glory which shall be revealed in us.
Romans 8:18

For our light affliction, which is but for a moment, is working for us a far more exceeding and eternal weight of glory, while we do not look at the things which are seen, but at the things which are not seen. For the things which are seen are temporary, but the things which are not seen are eternal.
II Corinthians 4:17,18

Thank You, dear Father, for Your faithfulness, goodness, and mercy that follows us all the days of our lives, and thank You that Your love is our constant companion Through every painful valley and struggle. Thank You for Your unquenchable joy that brings strength in the journey.

FIGHT FOR YOUR FAMILIES

Therefore I positioned men behind
the lower parts of the wall, at the openings;
and I set the people according to their families,
with their swords, their spears, and their
bows. And I looked, and arose and said to the
nobles, to the leaders, and to the rest of the
people, "Do not be afraid of them. Remember
the Lord, great and awesome, and fight for
your brethren, your sons, your daughters, your
wives, and your houses."
Nehemiah 4:13,14

*T*he book of *Nehemiah* is an encouraging and inspiring account of the difference one praying man can make in restoring and rebuilding the devastated, broken, and demolished walls of Jerusalem. This comparatively small book is filled with relevant truth for those of us who are presently fighting for our families and our culture.

The blatant tearing down of moral and biblical standards within my own lifetime is shocking to observe. The innocence and moral and spiritual strength of our children are being robbed by strong liberal and demonic influences being poured into this generation through the media, the educational systems, and even by parents who themselves have been brainwashed to believe that there are no absolute standards. We are living in a generation similar to that of the Judges where, "everyone did as he saw fit." (Judges 21:25)

What an amazing season it is in which to be alive and moving in the revival power and promises of God. Into these dark and perilous times God has promised to intervene on behalf of our families.

> *"For I will pour water on him who is thirsty, and floods on the dry ground; I will pour My Spirit on your descendants, and My blessing on your offspring; they will spring up among the grass like willows by the watercourses."*
> Isaiah 44:3,4

I can joyfully and painfully remember those demanding days of raising our own children. All three of our girls were born into not only a Christian home, but also a home in which both Charles and I were actively involved in ministry. Because we were young, inexperienced, and dealing with many of our own unhealed and unresolved inner wounds, we made many mistakes in parenting our beautiful girls. Yet today they each stand as women of God who love the Lord and their families. What did we learn about "fighting for our families?" We knew we loved our girls with all our hearts, but many times we were actually making it harder for them to fully embrace the ways of the Lord. As I cried out to the Lord, He showed me that to deal with my own inner wounds as a parent, and to honestly own up to my own failures was an important step in "fighting for our families." Learning how to humbly say, "Forgive me, I was wrong," became an important tool of healing for us. I began to study every book I could find on raising healthy, godly children. It soon became obvious that emotionally nurturing children with much attention and affection was absolutely essential. To learn how to create an atmosphere of warmth and laughter, filled with words of affirmation and appreciation, was even more vital than religiously obeying rules and commands.

Emotional nurturing prepared our children's hearts for spiritual nurturing. To teach the Word of the Lord both verbally and through example became very important. Providing them with wholesome and fun experiences and memories of church and fellowship became an important goal for us as parents. I remember one afternoon while in prayer, I heard God instruct me to hold each of my girls and declare over them their destiny in Him, "You were born to love, serve, and enjoy the Lord all the days of your life."

Someone jokingly told me one time that a mother never leaves the birthing table. Not only do we give natural birth, but all through life, we find ourselves in travail for life to come forth in our families. Paul seemed to have captured this concept in Galatians 4:19:

> *My little children, for whom I labor in birth*
> *again until Christ is formed in you. . . .*

One incident especially lingers in my memory bank. While away at school, we watched one of our daughters begin to make choices that we knew would lead only to despair and destruction for her. We knew that God has a destiny over her life, and the warfare was intense. Often, especially in the middle of the night, fear and anxiety gripped my heart on her behalf.

During those intense months of struggle for her, the Lord led me to study His Word for the promises He had given regarding our families and households. During one meeting, as the Spirit of the Lord began to powerfully move, I experienced such a strong cry of intercession for her that I thought my heart would break. I began to weep and sob with an unusual intensity. Even those around me were surprised by what they saw happening in me. But, I was interceding for her life and her destiny in God. The few who knew what was happening began to gather around me and enter with me into intense warfare praying.

I returned home pondering what all had happened. Imagine my delight as I read these words that week from both Jeremiah and Isaiah:

> *Thus says the LORD: "Refrain your voice from weeping, and your eyes from tears; for your work shall be rewarded, says the LORD, and they shall come back from the land of the enemy. There is hope in your future, says the LORD, that your children shall come back to their own border."*
> Jeremiah 31:16,17

*Shall the prey be taken from the mighty,
or the captives of the righteous be delivered?
But thus says the LORD: "Even the captives of
the mighty shall be taken away, and the prey of
the terrible be delivered; for I will contend with
him who contends with you, and I will save
your children."*
Isaiah 49:24,25

I then entered a season of praise and thanksgiving believing His promises. Even though things were not immediately different, something had been broken in the spiritual realm.

Now that our children are grown, strong intercession continues on their behalf, and on behalf of our grandchildren. In these perilous times, learning to pray prophetically and biblically over our families and our congregations is essential. Begin to daily proclaim:

My children are children of Covenant
*"As for Me," says the LORD, "this is My
covenant with them: My Spirit who is upon you,
and My words which I have put in your mouth,
shall not depart from your mouth, nor from
the mouth of your descendants, nor from the
mouth of your descendants' descendants," says
the LORD, "from this time and forevermore."*
Isaiah 59:21

My children are children of Promise
*"And it shall come to pass in the last days,
says God, that I will pour out of My Spirit on*

*all flesh; your sons and your daughters shall
prophesy, your young men shall see visions,
your old men shall dream dreams."*
Acts 2:17

*For the promise is to you and to your children,
and to all who are afar off, as many as the Lord
our God will call."*
Acts 2:39

My children are children of Peace
*All your children shall be taught by the LORD,
and great shall be the peace of your children.*
Isaiah 54:13

In the midst of the struggles and triumphs of our lives, we are growing stronger in His grace. Through it all we are learning how to trust Him and how to depend on His Word. For as long as we have breath we will "fight for our families," and learn to hold them, enjoy them, love them, and pray for them, regardless of their age!

Thank You, Father, that in spite of what we see with our natural eye, You are teaching us how to effectively fight for our families. We are confidently standing on Your promises that will never fail! According to Your promises, pour out Your Holy Spirit upon our children, grandchildren, and great-grandchildren. Lord, send revival into our families, churches and culture!

ENJOYING MY BELOVED

*Like an apple tree among the trees of the
woods, so is my beloved among the sons.
I sat down in his shade with great delight, and
his fruit was sweet to my taste. He brought me
to the banqueting house, and his banner over
me was love.*
Song of Songs 2:3,4

Never will I forget memorizing the first question of
the Westminster catechism. A group of us 11- and
12-year-olds sat in class obediently reciting together:
"What is the chief end of man? The chief end of man is
to glorify God and to enjoy Him forever." This was quite
a lofty theological concept for my young mind to grasp. I
wondered how I would explain what this 1st article of confession from the catechism really meant if I were called
upon by our dear Pastor Rost to do so.

Even though I was only 11 years old, I had already been
asking what my purpose in life really was. As I studied this
catechism statement my heart was especially fascinated
by the phrase: "to enjoy Him forever." I thought I could

understand that God wanted me to "follow all His rules" or else, but how does someone enjoy God?

Thus the Holy Spirit would shoot His arrow into my heart, and begin to shape both my destiny and journey with Him. The next year when I had a personal encounter with not only the Savior of the world, but with my personal, living, beloved Savior, never again would I be the same. One of the first things I discovered as a young believer was the power the words from the catechism were to have upon my life. I was determined to discover how to both glorify God and especially how to enjoy Him. Through the years it became increasingly clear that I would never really glorify Him if I didn't first thoroughly enjoy Him. But, how does one begin to learn to enjoy God, the creator of all the universe?

Over the years many Scriptures and many encounters with my Beloved Lord have taught me that learning to enjoy and delight in Him always begins with a revelation and personal experience of His deep, relentless love and enjoyment of us.

> *"Don't be afraid. Dear Zion, don't despair. Your*
> *God is present among you, a strong Warrior*
> *there to save you. Happy to have you back,*
> *he'll calm you with his love and delight you*
> *with his songs."*
> Zephaniah 3:17 The Message

*Behold what manner of love the Father has
bestowed on us, that we should be called
children of God!*
I John 3:1a,b

Learning to renew my mind by studying, meditating, and obeying His Word has changed my life and the way I think.

*And do not be conformed to this world, but
be transformed by the renewing of your mind,
that you may prove what is that good and
acceptable and perfect will of God.*
Romans 12:2

Soaking in His Presence and in His truth has brought revelation, healing, and joy into the deepest places of my soul.

*I've loved you the way my Father
has loved me. Make yourselves at home in my
love. If you keep my commands, you'll remain
intimately at home in my love. That's what
I've done—kept my Father's commands and
made myself at home in his love. I've told you
these things for a purpose: that my joy might
be your joy, and your joy wholly mature. This
is my command: Love one another the way I
loved you. This is the very best way to love. Put
your life on the line for your friends. You are
my friends when you do the things I command
you. I'm no longer calling you servants because
servants don't understand what their master*

is thinking and planning. No, I've named you
friends because I've let you in on everything
I've heard from the Father.
John 15:9-15 The Message

I am learning to obey Him even when I don't feel like it. Choosing to say, "Yes, Lord" when I am in a dark, discouraging season of life has been crucial in learning to enjoy Him!

"If you take away the yoke from your midst,
the pointing of the finger, and speaking
wickedness, if you extend your soul to the
hungry and satisfy the afflicted soul, then your
light shall dawn in the darkness, and your
darkness shall be as the noonday. The LORD
will guide you continually, and satisfy your soul
in drought, and strengthen your bones; you
shall be like a watered garden, and like a spring
of water, whose waters do not fail."
Isaiah 58:9b-11

I can clearly recall a season in my life when I was so discouraged and angry at the circumstances in which I found myself, that I plummeted into a deep depression. I surely wasn't fun to live with (one of my conference themes), and the Lord seemed very far away.

During this time I wouldn't read the Word or pray. I felt the ugly poison of self-pity seeping into my soul, and I began to isolate myself from others. (The amazing thing about all of this was that I knew better! I had repeatedly taught about these subjects, and was now sadly reaping the results of my own disobedience.)

However, early in my life with Him the Lord had absolutely ruined me with a dynamic encounter and experience of His life, love, and joyful Presence. He really had become my joy and hope in life.

Now you've got my feet on the life path, all
radiant from the shining of your face. Ever
since you took my hand, I'm on the right way.
Psalm 16:11 The Message

As the weeks passed, so did my deep loneliness for His Presence increase. In the midst of my tears of frustration, a yearning for Him and for the revelation of His Word painfully arose to the surface of my life. I knew to the core of my being that I loved Him more than the pain, anger, disappointments, and frustration presently swirling around my life.

One morning I walked into Charles' small office at the back of the house, and plopped down on a small hassock in the middle of the room. I sat there and sobbed. "I miss You. You win. I repent before You, and I yield to You. Even though I don't like what's happening, I bow my knee to Your sovereignty and to Your will." Instantly I encountered His presence. Oh, how I had missed Him!

Continuing to sit there, feelings of guilt and regret began to assail me. "Oh Lord, what do You really think of my actions and attitudes of these past weeks? I know You must really be grieved and disappointed in me." At that moment I opened the Scripture to Psalm 18. When my eyes came to verse 19, it jumped off the page deep into my heart.

> *He also brought me out into a broad place;*
> *He delivered me because He delighted in me.*
> Psalm 18:19

I struggled to accept this Word. How could the Lord delight in me when I had been such a failure? As I allowed His Word to fill my heart and mind, His love and cleansing washed over my bruised heart and soul. In that moment the mystery of His amazing grace and love became etched more deeply into the fabric of my life. He rescued me from my own foolishness because He delighted in me. Jesus is the Lover of our souls, and nothing shall ever separate us from the relentless love of God. He alone is our tremendous Lover. It is through the ongoing experience of receiving such love that we learn to enjoy Him and overflow with the fruit of life that will always glorify Him. Even when we don't deserve it, His love and grace relentlessly pursue us.

> *If you abide in Me, and My words*
> *abide in you, you will ask what you desire,*
> *and it shall be done for you. By this My Father*
> *is glorified, that you bear much fruit;*
> *so you will be My disciples.*
> John 15:7,8

Lord, we worship and adore You, and we lay our lives down before You. Thank you, Father, that as we learn to receive Your joy, delight, and love for us, our love, delight, and enjoyment of You increases. We live to glorify You and to enjoy You forever.

RELUCTANT GIVER

But this I say: He who sows sparingly will also reap sparingly, and he who sows bountifully will also reap bountifully. So let each one give as he purposes in his heart, not grudgingly or of necessity; for God loves a cheerful giver. And God is able to make all grace abound toward you, that you, always having all sufficiency in all things, may have an abundance for every good work.
2 Corinthians 9:6-8

*H*aving just returned from church, I ran into the kitchen to answer the phone. I wondered who would be calling so late. When I answered, I heard my mom's voice calling from Florida, "Where have you been? I've been calling all night. Your aunt is in the Coney Island Hospital. What are you going to do about it?" We talked some more, but when I hung up the phone, I simply stood in the kitchen sensing that my life was about to drastically change. I had taught about the changing seasons of life, but wasn't sure this was a change I wanted to readily embrace.

Within the next few months, Charles and I found our-selves back in New York City closing up not only one house, but two. For not only would we be moving my aunt to Maryland, but Nana, Charles' mom now also needed to be cared for. Closing up two homes that had been lived in for more than 40 years was quite overwhelming. Even more challenging was having both of our loved ones move in with us. Especially since I had just re-arranged my whole house to provide more space for quiet medita-tion and study, this proved to be quite a disruptive change to my plans. Laura and Dianna were both away at school, but Jenny was just in Middle School. I soon learned that I was part of what is known as the "sandwich generation." Charles and I were between needing to meet the needs of an older generation and a younger generation. During those next years, I remember often feeling like a big choc-olate chip cookie with everyone wanting a bite.

Since both Nana and my aunt had health issues, the first few weeks were spent in and out of the doctor's office. I soon realized that I needed to take a sabbatical from my staff responsibilities at church, the daily radio program I had been doing, and my conference schedule. None of this did I do willingly, for I thoroughly enjoyed what I was doing. It just didn't seem fair. After all, wasn't I fruitfully serving the Lord? Now I became almost as housebound as my precious loved ones. Soon little seeds of resentment found fertile soil in my disgruntled heart.

When you serve others under a sense of obligation and duty, you soon lose your joy and enthusiasm. All the changes and unexpected added work also began taking a toll on my health, my blood pressure rose, and I was developing insomnia. So much for having quiet time to seek the Lord for revival!!

One afternoon as I stopped briefly in the church office, numbers of people commented on how exhausted and tired I was looking. Out of love and concern for me I was told: "Dotty, you really need to take care of yourself." My first response was to want to shout back, "And how am I suppose to do that?" But of course, I was the senior pastor's wife and such loss of control was not acceptable behavior. So, instead I internalized my anger and frustration and became even more depressed and discouraged.

When I arrived home, I took a few more minutes to be alone with the Lord to have a "pity party." As I cried tears of anger and frustration, I repeatedly asked, "Lord, how do I take care of myself? Don't You care how tired I am?" As I finally became quiet before Him, I heard: "My daughter, you don't need to take care of yourself right now, but you need to die to yourself." "What? That couldn't be You, Lord; what do You mean, 'die to yourself'?"

> *I am crucified with Christ: nevertheless I live;*
> *yet not I, but Christ liveth in me: and the life*
> *which I now live in the flesh I live by the faith*
> *of the Son of God, who loved me, and gave*
> *himself for me.*
> Galatians 2:20 KJV

So there I was once again enduring the pruning knife of the Lord I loved. That afternoon as both my aunt and Nana were taking a nap, the skillful surgeon was cutting into the dark places of my soul. Clearly I heard: "This is a time for you to die to your own rights, to your own schedule, to your own privacy, and to your own control of your life." The Lord and I struggled with these issues all afternoon. He put His finger upon the resentment, anger, and rebellion which was growing in my heart. In fact the struggle to totally surrender everything to Him actually lasted for a number of weeks. But, as everyone who lives in an abiding relationship with Him soon learns, resistance and disobedience both grieve and quench the work of His Spirit within us. Soon the stand-off between the Lord and me became unbearable. I still remember bowing my knee to Him one afternoon and saying, "OK, Lord, You win. I surrender my heart, my rights, my schedule, my plans, even my dreams for Your Kingdom to You. Your will, not mine be done." I wish I could say that this was a once and for all joyous transaction, but to be honest, I found myself being brought repeatedly to this place of "death to self" during those 12 years of caring for four precious loved ones, and at times, most exasperating family members. (During that same year I became legal guardian of my uncle who lived in Florida, and also assumed more responsibility for my beloved mom.)

It is very noteworthy to recount a most significant happening just weeks after this "surrender time." Two compassionate and sensitive women came to me and volunteered their services to help care for our loved ones. Both Lona and Jean would become a source of help, comfort, and encouragement to us as a family for the next few years. Thank God for those in His church who have the anointed ministry of helps and encouragement.

It was soon after this that I heard Him quietly whisper into my heart, "And now, My daughter, I will show you how to take care of yourself, for I am still the Shepherd who restores your soul." In the following months I took a class on "gerontology" (caring for the elderly), and discovered the value of support groups for care-givers. Charles and I also learned the value of mini-dates, vacations, and making time for joy and laughter!

All four of my loved ones are now in the hands of our Lord, and I can look back upon one of the most demanding and fruitful season of my life with deep gratitude in my heart. I have learned that He loves a cheerful giver not only regarding our money, but in all of our service to Him, whether it be in preaching, praying, or preparing a meal for our elderly!

Thank You, Lord, for teaching us the ways of Your heart in every circumstance of life, and thank You for Your amazing grace!

OVERWHELMED

From the end of the earth I will cry to You,
when my heart is overwhelmed; lead me to the
rock that is higher than I. For You have been a
shelter for me, a strong tower from the enemy.
Psalm 61:2,3

I slammed the bedroom door and sank into my "prayer chair" and sobbed. I felt totally overwhelmed, helpless, and alone. The responsibility of caring for four of my precious elderly family members, being a wife and mother, the senior pastor's wife and co-pastor, was just too much! Furthermore, we were in the middle of a powerful move of God, people were coming from all over to participate and receive from the Lord's bounty, and I was locked in my bedroom sobbing from frustration and exhaustion.

In the midst of those awesome gatherings with my house full of people, Nana fell from her chair at the breakfast table with a stroke. My mom watched in fear and anxiety as the paramedics came, and in the midst of much prayer and panic, we rushed her to the hospital. Then the next morning as my mom awakened, she cried out with severe pain in her back. It was early Sunday morning and we were preparing for services. Instead of the revival meeting, I rushed Mom to the emergency room in the same hospital where Nana was.

As the day progressed, and Charles and the family came in and out of the hospital in between our services, I found myself going from the emergency room with Mom to the third floor with Nana. As evening approached, both my mom and mother-in-law had been admitted to the hospital. I was emotionally and physically drained and spiritually overwhelmed. "My God, we're in the middle of a powerful move of Your Spirit; have You forgotten me? Where are You in all of this?"

It was the next morning that found me sobbing in my "prayer chair." Almost immediately Psalm 61 filled my mind and heart: ". . .when my heart is overwhelmed lead me to the Rock that is higher than I." "Lord, I am over-whelmed and I don't know what it practically means to be led to the Rock that is higher than I!" As I became quiet and still, His gentle voice became life to me. "My child, you feel as if you're sinking in your circumstances. Look up, My hand is there to lift you up higher into My Pres-ence, and to place your feet firmly on the Rock of your salvation. I am your stability and safety in the midst of turbulence. I am your refuge and your strong tower."

I don't know how long I sat there, but when I returned to the kitchen, and to all the present demands of my life, I knew my Lord had once again met me in the quiet of the secret place of His Presence and in the power of His Word. Once again, He had strengthened and refreshed me by

His Holy Spirit. He also gave me a strategy not only for coping with the stress, but also learning how to become stronger because of it.

Slowly I learned what things were restorative to me. Even brief times of total quiet, learning to deeply breathe in His Presence, and worshipfully speaking the name of Jesus imparted new strength to me. Learning to peacefully talk to Him as I was cooking, cleaning, driving, or sitting in doctors' offices became another source of rest and spiritual strength to me.

> *Be anxious for nothing, but in everything by prayer and supplication, with thanksgiving, let your requests be made known to God; and the peace of God, which surpasses all understanding, will guard your hearts and minds through Christ Jesus.*
> Philippians 4:6,7

I was also learning that laughter and a sense of humor greatly helped to relieve stress and tension. Increasingly, my time with my precious ones became filled with funny stories from the past. We were learning together to exchange our murmurings into laughter. (This worked most of the time.)

How clearly I remember the morning when both my aunt and mother-in-law slowly shuffled into the kitchen. Both were complaining that they were dying. As this continued for awhile, I finally turned to them, and with great intensity declared, "No one is dying in this house today!" They, as well as I, were so stunned that we just stood in the kitchen looking at one another. Then my mother-in-law with a smile on her face said, "OK." At that, all three of us laughed and enjoyed the rest of the day.

*A merry heart does good, like medicine, but a
broken spirit dries the bones.*
Proverbs 17:22

Then I learned how to ask for more prayer covering, and for more practical help from those who could help care for my loved ones. The challenges of life did not decrease; in fact in many ways they increased, but I had changed. His grace is sufficient, and He taught me more deeply how to receive more of His love, joy, and peace in the midst of the challenges of life!

Thank You, Father, that when life becomes overwhelming and confusing, You reach down, deep into our spirits and lift us up to stand on the Rock of our salvation. We love You!

DIVINE APPOINTMENT

Trust in the LORD with all your heart, and lean
not on your own understanding; in all your
ways acknowledge Him, and He shall direct
your paths.
Proverbs 3:5-6

*M*y heart leapt with excitement as I pondered the invitation to attend a women's leadership round-table. There were only twelve of us invited, and we each were published authors and national speakers. We were being called together to discuss relevant issues pertaining to women in leadership. What an opportunity to learn, but I had only one problem. I was still in the midst of my care-giving season and our precious Nana, who had been living with us for 7½ years, had recently suffered a serious stroke which now left her unconscious in a nursing home. The stress of those days lay heavily upon us as a family.

Lord, what do I do? What is Your will? Do I go to the roundtable and stay away for 24 hours or do I stay home? During these years of caring for my elderly, it seemed as if I was often in this valley of indecision. I thought of the Scripture in Proverbs 16:9:

> *A man's heart plans his way, but the LORD*
> *directs his steps.*

My constant prayer was, Lord, I yield to You. You direct and guide my path. Show me what to do! Direct my paths!

As Charles and I prayerfully discussed the invitation, we both had a deep peace that I was to attend. That decision would prove to be a strategic time for me. During those brief hours around the roundtable, God gave us the gift of friendship that would be useful for His purposes for the revival years ahead.

The discussions and fellowship were deeply enriching and inspiring. It once again became clear to me that cultivating godly friendships and relationships was one of the richest gifts He bestows on us as His children. One of the women attending was Mary Audrey Raycroft from the Airport Fellowship in Toronto. The outpouring of the Father's love in the midst of this precious fellowship led by John and Carol Arnott was destined to impact the church world-wide. Quickly, Mary Audrey and I discovered a bond of unity and love between us in our quest for the glory of His revival Presence. Before this event concluded, we both knew we would be ministering together. The other woman of God who deeply influenced and impacted my life in those hours was Dr. Fuschia Pickett. Dr. Fuschia, as a number of us respectfully addressed her, had been influencing my life for a number of years. I had known her and received much from her teaching, especially during some powerful leadership retreats that Iverna Tompkins had called together, but these hours were especially meaningful for me personally.

In the midst of the lively discussions, I was quietly called out of the room. One of the sisters put her arms around me and told me that a call had just come for me to immediately call home. I just knew that Nana had passed into the Presence of the Lord. As Charles and I spoke together we both felt that this was a bittersweet moment. Nana was now free from her physical pain and enjoying the Lord, but we felt the pain of her loss. When I reentered the room and shared that I would need to return home, my tears began to flow. The love and support that poured from these women to me brought deep comfort and healing to my heart. Dr. Fuschia placed her hands on me and prayed for an eternal perspective to be given. As I drove home I took with me an impartation of His grace and comfort that would be a permanent deposit in my life.

Soon, a phone call came from Mary Audrey asking me to share as a speaker in her women's conference, "Releasers of Life," and thus began one of the most enriching and significant times of my life. Also, at this conference was Brenda Kilpatrick from the Brownsville revival in Pensacola, Florida. The atmosphere in the room during those days was saturated with the Lord's Presence and love. In a deeper way all of us were learning to "soak" in the Father's love and personal affection for each of us.

During the session in which I spoke, I experienced a deeper and richer anointing than I had previously known.

It became obvious that His grace and anointing also rested heavily upon those who were in attendance. The hunger within their hearts pulled and drew from the rivers of life within me. And this was happening with each speaker. A Scripture comes to mind which helps us understand how hunger and thirst for Him leads us to feasting and drinking from Him:

They are abundantly satisfied with the fullness of Your house, and You give them drink from the river of Your pleasures. For with You is the fountain of life; in Your light we see light.
Psalm 36:8,9

When I finally returned to my seat, Brenda turned to me and said, "I want you to come to Brownsville and bring the same message, and bring the same dance team with you." A group of about 25 dancers had accompanied me from Immanuel's Church. As they ministered unto the Lord in dance with banners and flags, the anointing of His Presence increased within that room. Those were days of a greater impartation of His righteousness, joy, and peace into each of our hearts. When one is in His manifest loving Presence, change, transformation, and healing will always result.

In those few days together, divine appointments were sovereignly arranged for many of us.

Personally experiencing both the Toronto and Brownsville revivals of the 90s will always be some of the greatest honors and privileges of my life. Soon I became part of a team of four led by Brenda Kilpatrick. We travelled to many places around America, as well as into Mexico, England, Wales, Ireland, and Scotland.

As a team we learned to laugh, cry, minister, and defer to one another. We were always prepared to share His Word, but if we sensed someone also carried His heart for the hour we would gladly yield to that one. At times all four of us shared. To experience such a flow of life and unity released even more of the Father's pleasure upon us.

On one occasion as we were ministering in England, we were each asked to share our revival experiences over the years. Never will I forget that afternoon! As we passed the microphone from one to another, the weight of His glory and Presence became stronger and stronger. The atmosphere became so charged with His Presence that people came into the room from all over the building. Eventually we all either sat, lay on the floor on our faces, or knelt in quiet adoration of the Lord who chose to make Himself beautifully manifest to us that day.

He who has My commandments and keeps them, it is he who loves Me. And he who loves Me will be loved by My Father, and I will love him and manifest Myself to him.
John 14:21

Amazingly, it was only recently that I received an e-mail from some missionaries staying in a remote village in India. They recounted that in deep discouragement they stopped in a village to seek the Lord. Even in that rather primitive environment they were able to get a few channels on the local TV, one of which was the Christian channel that had recorded that anointed afternoon in England. A number of years later those precious folks wrote that as they watched and listened, the glory of God's Presence came into their small room. They were set free from their discouragement and freshly filled with His love. How absolutely incredible are the ways of the Lord!

Cast your bread upon the waters, for you will
find it after many days.
Ecclesiastes 11:1

As I look back upon those profound days of flowing in a fresh river of life and revelation, I am even hungrier for the glory of His Presence to be manifest today and in the days to come. I believe He has given us a taste of heaven to motivate us to participate with Him in prayer, fasting, and prophetic proclamation for the greatest harvest this earth has ever experienced.

Sow for yourselves righteousness; reap in
mercy; break up your fallow ground, For it is
time to seek the LORD, till He comes and rains
righteousness on you.
Hosea 10:12

God is still setting up divine appointments for each of us. He is still guiding us to cultivate godly friendships and relationships with those who will together with us cry for "His kingdom to come on earth as it is in heaven."

Thank You, Father, for the sheer joy and delight of knowing You, loving You and serving You! And thank You for the godly, edifying, and enjoyable relationship You have prepared for us in our journey of serving Your purposes for this generation. May we always be alert to those divine appointments You are always preparing for us.

Is There a Song in the House?

*Shout joyfully to the Lord, all the earth; break
forth in song, rejoice and sing praises.*
Psalm 98:4

*S*inging and shouting unto the Lord is a powerful biblical theme. Repeatedly we are admonished to:

*Sing to the Lord a new song! Sing to the Lord,
all the earth. Sing to the Lord, bless His name;
proclaim the good news of His salvation from
day to day.*
Psalm 96:1,2 NIV

Even Paul, in the midst of his profound proclamations
of truth, understood the place and power of song in tri-
umphantly living the Spirit-filled life.

*. . .be filled with the Spirit, speaking to one
another in psalms* and hymns and spiritual
songs, singing and making melody in your
heart to the Lord. . . .
Ephesians 5:18b,19

To live a Spirit-filled life is to overflow in song, praise, and thanksgiving. It is to enter His gates with gratitude and His courts with praise.

Recently as I pondered the place of music, song, dance, and praise in the furtherance of the work of the kingdom here on earth, I sighed before the Lord. "Father, why is it that I find it much easier to grumble, complain, and whine when life and circumstances get difficult, than I do to sing, shout, and praise?" As I continued my study of biblical praise and song, I realized I had much yet to apply to my daily life on this subject.

From my studies over the years I learned that even in normal conversation about 80% of what we say is negative, critical, or complaining. Have you ever really listened to how people speak to one another, especially in families? It is also reliably reported that it actually takes eight positive comments to undo two negative ones. It is not surprising then that the Scriptures have so much to say about the power of the tongue.

Death and life are in the
power of the tongue. . . .
Proverbs 18:21a

There is one who speaks like
the piercings of a sword, but the tongue of the
wise promotes health.
Proverbs 12:18

With it we bless our God and Father, and with
it we curse men, who have been made in the

> *similitude of God. Out of the same mouth*
> *proceed blessing and cursing. My brethren,*
> *these things ought not to be so."*
> James 3:9,10

In the midst of this study on the power of the tongue and the power of a song and shout to the Lord, He gave me a visual picture. During a time of corporate praise, I saw the atmosphere around us filled with a haze of darkness, heaviness, and confusion, and then I saw a bottle of glass cleaner! As the contents of the bottle were applied to the heavy atmosphere, things became brighter, cleaner, and more peaceful. I smiled at the picture, and while inquiring of the Lord, I heard, "The more you give to Me the shout of triumph and the song of praise, the more the enemy will withdraw. Praise actually cleans the atmosphere." Almost immediately a number of passages filled my mind with fresh illumination and understanding. What I was learning about the power of the song of praise was changing my life and my prayers. I also received a clearer eternal perspective.

2 Chronicles 20 is a most intriguing study on the strangeness of the Lord's strategy for battle. Who ever heard of putting the choir at the head of the army? Who would have imagined that we could actually change and shape events through the power of prayer, prophetic declaration, and the shout and song of praise and thanksgiving? All of this would remain quite illogical, if it were not for this deep biblical truth:

> *Finally, my brethren, be strong in the Lord*
> *and in the power of His might. Put on the*

*whole armor of God that you may be able to
stand against the wiles of the devil.
For we do not wrestle against flesh and blood,
but against principalities, against powers,
against the rulers of the darkness of this age,
against spiritual hosts of wickedness in the
heavenly places.*
Ephesians 6:10-12

*For though we walk in the flesh, we do not war
according to the flesh. For the weapons of our
warfare are not carnal but mighty in God for
pulling down of strongholds. . . .*
II Corinthians 10:3,4

Because we are fighting a spiritual battle, He gives us the powerful weapons of song, praise, and prophetic declaration to wage war in the heavenly places.

In II Chronicles 20, we are caught up in an intense drama in the history of Israel. A "vast army" was coming up against King Jehoshaphat and the people of God. The king called for a time of fasting and prayer, and the prophets were moved upon to give inspiration and direction:

*. . ."Do not be afraid nor dismayed
because of this great multitude,
for the battle is not yours, but God's."*
II Chronicles 20:15

In this atmosphere of prayer, praise, worship, and prophetic proclamation, Jehoshaphat received a strategy from heaven:

*And when he had consulted with the people,
he appointed those who should sing to the
LORD, and who should praise the beauty of
holiness, as they went out before the army and
were saying: "Praise the LORD, for His mercy
endures forever."*
II Chronicles 20:21

And amazingly:

*Now when they began to sing and to praise,
the LORD set ambushes against the people of
Ammon, Moab, and Mount Seir, who had come
against Judah; and they were defeated.*
II Chronicles 20:22

It is as the people of God sing and praise and make declaration that our God is good, that confusion and division comes into the enemy's camp. But God is not only desirous for us to win the battle; He wants to make us "more than conquerors." The people went into the enemy's camp and took so much plunder that it took them more than the three days to collect it all. This is a profound truth; the song of the Lord makes us "more than conquerors." We not only defeat the enemy, we go into his camp and take back what he has stolen from us.

In Acts 16 Paul and Silas gave us another demonstration of the power of the song of praise. From dynamically preaching the Gospel and being vessels used to bring the word of salvation and deliverance to Philippi, they were wrongfully arrested, "severely flogged," and then put into chains and thrown into prison. What a way to treat God's servants! Imagine yourself in this situation. How would you feel? What would you do? I failed each of these questions. My next question was, what motivated Paul and Silas, bloodied, tired, and obviously unjustly treated, to break out in praying and singing? I believe Paul himself gives us some insight:

> *. . .while we do not look at the things which are*
> *seen, but at the things which are not seen. For*
> *the things which are seen are temporary, but*
> *the things which are not seen are eternal.*
> II Corinthians 4:18

When we are able to see into the spiritual realities, when we "fix our eyes on Jesus," and not on the immediate circumstances, we will also break out in prayer, praise, and song. And, as the other prisoners were listening (for there are always others listening to our words), something extraordinary happened! A *suddenly* of God occurred. Prayer and praise will always release God's *suddenly*. Everything shook loose, and everyone's chains fell off. Once again we see that prayer and praise are not meant to only bring us personal breakthrough victory, but they will always impact others. With great joy the jailer and his whole family were birthed into God's Kingdom, and the church of Philippi was well on its way.

> *So they said, "Believe on the Lord*
> *Jesus Christ, and you will be saved,*
> *you and your household."*
> Acts 16:31

Father, thank You for the most unusual and yet powerful weapon of song, prayer, and praise. May our lives and homes be filled with songs of the Lord! And the shout of triumph!

GOD'S INTERRUPTIONS

And having come in, the angel said to her,
"Rejoice, highly favored one, the Lord is with
you; blessed are you among women!"
Luke 1:28

*I*t didn't take me long as a believer in Jesus to realize that to find favor with God can at times be quite scary. To love Him, with all our heart, all our soul, and all our mind means He has the absolute right to turn our lives upside down, and to change all our normal dreams. Little do we initially realize the implication of saying "Yes, Lord."

The study of both the lives of Elizabeth and Mary found in the Gospel of Luke yields wonderful treasures of understanding into the often bewildering ways of the Lord. When God sets His heart and choice upon someone, He usually completely interrupts their normal, accepted routine of living. Thank God for people throughout history who have been willing to leave the safety and security of the ordinary in order to embrace the often wild and risky purposes of an extraordinary God, whose only assurances to us are, "I love you," "I will never leave or forsake you," and "Trust me."

Zechariah and Elizabeth are an example of a couple who were tested, tried, and who seem to have finally settled for a normal life of unanswered prayer for a child. Then, when it was beyond all natural hope, the Lord decided to suddenly interrupt their lives with the intrusion of an unexpected, supernatural event. Both of these precious people were devout servants of the Lord, belonging to the religious order of the day and faithfully serving Him, (in spite of what I suspect was a deep wound in their hearts regarding being childless).

In the midst of Zechariah's serving his allotted time as priest in the temple, the emotional roller-coaster began – an angel appeared to him! Zechariah and Elizabeth's lives would never again be the same! The angelic announcement is definitely worth pondering:

> *But the angel said to him, "Do not be afraid, Zacharias, for your prayer is heard; and your wife Elizabeth will bear you a son, and you shall call his name John. And you will have joy and gladness, and many will rejoice at his birth.*
> Luke 1:13,14

My first response to the angel's announcement, "your prayer has been heard," is well, it's about time! I wondered if Elizabeth and Zechariah were still asking or had they just settled into the disappointment? After all, they were now quite old. But, since the Lord lives outside of our time parameters, and His timing is everything – their prayer was now being answered.

I was especially intrigued with the statement:

He will be a joy and delight to you,
and many will rejoice because of his birth.
Luke 1:14 NIV

What a wonderful insight into the heart of our God. Elizabeth's barrenness, especially in the culture of that day, undoubtedly brought much sorrow and tears to that faithful couple. Especially for Elizabeth, I wonder what she felt every month when her hopes were once again dashed. How did she feel when all those women around her gave birth to child after child, filling their home with joy and laughter? I can imagine that many a night passed with Elizabeth quietly weeping with grief in Zechariah's arms. Then finally the time came when both of these servants of the Lord acknowledged that now in the natural all hope was gone. Yet nothing misses the eyes of the Lord! He saw that even in their heartbreak, Elizabeth would continue to be upright and faithful to him. Now finally, in His perfect timing, their mourning would be turned into dancing. He would fill both their mouths and their home with laughter. How tender and compassionate are the Lord's ways: "He will be a joy and delight to you," is told them. One can only imagine how their little boy filled their hearts to overflowing! Our Father, even in accomplishing His greater plans and purposes on earth, is always personally interested in each one of us. He is intent upon healing our hearts and restoring a joyful dance to our lives, even as He brings forth a great prophet such as John the Baptist to serve His eternal purposes.

At the same time that Zechariah and Elizabeth's lives were being drastically interrupted in their later years, even more so was the life of a young ordinary country girl being turned upside down. Whenever angels get involved you can be assured that things will never again be the same. Imagine if you were Mary. You are young, recently engaged, and just full of dreams and excitement for your new life with a good husband, home, and family. Then seemingly out of nowhere an angel appears to Mary:

> *Rejoice, highly favored one, the Lord is with you; blessed are you among women!*
> Luke 1:28

The word favor implies acceptance, approval, and pleasure, but Mary seemingly wasn't yet taking in the fact that she was highly favored. Her initial reaction was one of fear, perplexity, and she was "greatly troubled." Who wouldn't react this way? The angelic announcement was to become even more intense and amazing – she would become pregnant by divine overshadowing:

> *And the angel answered and said to her, "The Holy Spirit will come upon you, and the power of the Highest will overshadow you; therefore, also, that Holy One who is to be born will be called the Son of God."*
> Luke 1:35

How could such "good news" for the world initially bring such pain, confusion, and turmoil into the life of a young, innocent girl, who found herself favored and chosen and thrust into a scandalous situation?

Mary was obviously an amazing young woman. I can't help but wonder what the Lord saw in her that caused Him to choose her above all others to bring into the world the most precious gift of His Son. I wonder how much of the angel's profound words Mary really understood:

"And behold, you will conceive in your womb and bring forth a Son, and shall call His name Jesus. He will be great, and will be called the Son of the Highest; and the Lord God will give Him the throne of His father David. And He will reign over the house of Jacob forever, and of His kingdom there will be no end."
Luke 1:31-33

One thing I do know, Mary's example of loving obedience and submission to the will of God, regardless of the personal pain and sacrifice it would introduce to her own private life, is an extraordinary jewel of beauty to behold in all of the biblical writings. Mary was a "Yes, Lord," woman!

Then Mary said, "Behold the maidservant of the Lord! Let it be to me according to your word." And the angel departed from her.
Luke 1:38

Mary's life would never again be normal. Often in her earthly journey she would experience the power of Simeon's words to her:

> Then Simeon blessed them, and said to Mary
> His mother, "Behold, this Child is destined for
> the fall and rising of many in Israel, and for a
> sign which will be spoken against (yes, a sword
> will pierce through your own soul also), that
> the thoughts of many hearts may be revealed."
> Luke 2:34,35

Mary would not only experience extraordinary favor, but she would also know a deep sword of pain piercing her own heart. Mary, along with numerous hosts of God's treasured men and women of faith, would learn that to love Him will at times wound our own hearts.

How thankful I am for those whom God can trust to stand true and faithful to Him, even when a sword pierces their own souls, and who lovingly, even if in great perplexity, accept the sudden interruptions of God into their lives, knowing that resurrection always follows death!

> For I consider that the sufferings of this present
> time are not worthy to be compared with the
> glory which shall be revealed in us.
> Romans 8:18

Thank You, Lord, for the beauty of who You are, and for the extraordinary ways You employ to win the hearts of men and women to utter and complete devotion to Yourself.

CHANGED BY 9/11

*"For nation will rise against nation,
and kingdom against kingdom.
And there will be famines, pestilences,
and earthquakes in various places.
All these are the beginning of sorrows."*
Matthew 24:7,8

*I*t was Tuesday morning, and as usual I was rushing about to get to our weekly Women's Bible study, "Titus II." As I was getting ready to walk out the door, the phone rang. It was my daughter, Laura. Since Laura had just given birth to our precious twins, Dylan and Brooke, on the first of September, and since she also had a seventeen-month-old, Kai, I knew I had to answer and see how she was. "Mom, I don't know what this is, but a plane just hit one of the twin towers." I remember commenting that this was a terrible accident to occur. I told Laura I had to go to the study, but would see her later when I came to help her with the three babies.

I walked into the Fellowship Hall where almost 100 women gathered each week from many different churches. This was a wonderful group of hungry, mature women of God, and we had really learned to love and encourage one another over the years. Getting ready to begin our study, I was praying when one of our Pastors ran into the room, pushing a TV and said something terrible was happening, and we needed to pray. Everything stopped in the room, and our attention was riveted to the TV screen. We were only miles from the White House and the Pentagon, and fear was beginning to fill the room.

Almost everyone in the room had family, friends, or acquaintances working in New York City, the Pentagon, or in Washington, DC. As we watched the shocking events unfold that morning of 9/11/2001, the room began to be filled with fear, panic, and turmoil. Numbers of women ran out into the parking lot to call family members and close friends on their cell phones, but virtually all cell service had been interrupted. As we re-gathered, the call to prayer was issued.

Never will I forget the nearly tangible atmosphere of fear filling the room. We were virtually immobilized by fear, panic, and confusion. Desperately, I stood up in front of my beloved sisters in the Lord and cried out to Him for a rhema word from Him on this situation. Almost immediately I heard; "Psalm 46, and Ellen has a word." I had seen Ellen earlier standing in the back of the room, but when I opened my eyes she was standing next to me. I then knew that He was determined, in those moments, to share His heart with us. I slowly and deliberately read from Psalm 46 (NIV):

> *God is our refuge and strength, an ever-present help in trouble. Therefore we will not fear,*

*though the earth give way and the mountains
fall into the heart of the sea, though its waters
roar and foam and the mountains quake with
their surging. There is a river whose streams
make glad the city of God, the holy place where
the Most High dwells. God is within her, she
will not fall; God will help her at break of day.
Nations are in uproar, kingdoms fall; he lifts
his voice, the earth melts. The LORD Almighty
is with us; the God of Jacob is our fortress.
Come and see what the LORD has done, the
desolations he has brought on the earth. He
makes wars cease to the ends of the earth.
He breaks the bow and shatters the spear;
he burns the shields with fire. He says, "Be
still, and know that I am God; I will be exalted
among the nations, I will be exalted in the
earth." The LORD Almighty is with us; the God
of Jacob is our fortress.*

These powerful words seemed to leap from the page. Because of who our God is, our *refuge* and our *strength* and an *ever present help in time of trouble*, **we will not fear**. As His truth was being proclaimed and believed, He cast out the fear. Even when we watched the "earth give way" as those twin towers horrifically collapsed, He admonished us to, "Be still and know that I am God." It is impressive to note that this powerful Psalm begins with earthquakes and all sorts of physical upheavals, and concludes with, "Be still and know that I am God." During the next weeks, this particular Psalm was read and reread on the radio, on TV and in the halls of Congress. It was also read by President Obama on the 10th anniversary of

9/11. It seemed as if the Lord gave this precious Psalm to America to both comfort and admonish us to put our trust in Him. "Lord, help us!"

When I finished reading Psalm 46, I gave the microphone to Ellen, knowing she heard a word from the Lord. She almost apologetically gave it saying it was only one simple phrase from Nehemiah 8:10c: "The joy of the Lord is your strength." It was the Lord reminding us who He is, and who we are as His children in these dark days. It was He who was reminding us that regardless of these sorrowful and horrendous events, our joy would remain because we are in intimate relationship with Him, and He has a purpose and plan that He will fulfill, and He has given us a sure and certain promise:

> *"Then the sign of the Son of Man will appear*
> *in heaven, and then all the tribes of the earth*
> *will mourn, and they will see the Son of Man*
> *coming on the clouds of heaven with power*
> *and great glory."*
> Matthew 24:30

That afternoon, helping my daughter care for her three precious babies, I was to receive another nugget of revelation into His heart. As we busily fed, changed, and cared for our three beautiful babies, Laura and I had the TV on, but without the sound. We both didn't want the sounds of such evil and suffering to even come into the atmosphere where our three innocent babies were. As Laura finished caring for the twins, she put Brooke into one of my arms and Dylan into the other. As I held them close to me, tears freely fell while I watched these terrible events unfold on the TV screen. Soon both babies fell asleep, beautiful, innocent, and filled with life. I felt I wanted to just hold them and always protect them from a world having gone crazy with hate and turmoil. Laura, observing that the babies were now sound asleep in my arms, offered to take them and put them into their beds. I looked up at her and said, "No, no, let me continue to hold them. Having them peacefully snuggle in my arms brings such comfort to my heart." As I said these words to Laura, I heard my Father's voice, "And even so do you bring comfort to My own heart, as you draw near and rest in my arms. For I too, weep at the events of today. I, too, grieve at the pain and sorrow of my creation." As I felt His Presence draw near and encompass me, a Scripture came to mind of Jesus weeping. And even though it was spoken to Israel as a nation, it is also relevant to us as a nation:

> *Now as He drew near, He saw the city and wept over it, saying, "If you had known, even you, especially in this your day, the things that make for your peace! But now they are hidden from your eyes."*
> Luke 19:41,42

As I held our precious 11-day-old twins in my arms, my own heart cried out, "Lord Jesus, may we as a nation not miss our own day of visitation. May we not fall asleep, dull and ignorant to all the signs around us of Your soon return. Give us a tender, repentant heart. Lord Jesus, have mercy upon us as a church and a nation." – May we never forget the lessons of 9/11!

AND THEN THERE WERE THREE
By Laura Schmitt Uecker

*There is an appointed time for everything. And
there is a time for every event under heaven. A
time to give birth. . . .*
Ecclesiastes 3:1

My husband and I met in college. We had many
things in common including a mutual feeling
that we weren't cut out to have children. Four years of
dating and 12 years of marriage later, my middle sister,
Dianna, gave birth to the first Schmitt grandchild. I was
so relieved all during her pregnancy – the pressure was
off! But something happened in that maternity ward as
George and I marveled at our newborn nephew, Chase. I
remember turning towards my husband suggesting that
we should try for one month to see if maybe God wanted
us to have children.

Our oldest son was born 9 months later, and soon after
we had twins. In 17 months we went from zero to three
babies.

You may be thinking, so what is the big deal? And for some, it probably wouldn't be. But for me, someone who never really thought about having children, who enjoyed a successful career and travel all over the world, this was a very big deal. What was God doing? What happened to my well-organized life? I felt I didn't even have a natural maternal instinct – help! What had I done?

As I write this, my oldest son, Kai, is now 11 and our twins, Dylan and Brooke, are 10. I am happy to report that mom, dad, and kids are happy, healthy, and thriving. I look back on the last decade and marvel at all the Lord has done. I'd like to share three lessons this journey has taught me so far.

"Remember the words of the Lord Jesus,
that He Himself said, 'It is more blessed to give
than to receive.'"
Acts 20:35

I grew up with this Bible verse. Given my family dynamics, and watching first-hand my parents live this out on a daily basis, it was an easy one for me. Of course it is more blessed to give than to receive, but what happens when the tables are turned and you are on the receiving end?

I didn't know I was carrying twins until I was six months along. My daughter somehow was missed on the first two sonograms. The night before my third sonogram I remember telling George that there has to be two in there, or else we were having one huge baby. Sure enough, the next day two heads popped up on the screen. The joy, elation, excitement of hearing the news (twins do not run in our family) was quickly replaced with dire predictions. Since I was older and carrying multiples, now the concern was that something was amiss. I was put on full-time bed rest – not exactly easy with a 14-month-old running around, but something amazing happened. Our church and family not only surrounded us with overwhelming prayer, but they took care of us on a practical level. They helped take care of our son, brought us meals on a daily basis, went food shopping for us, and even took turns cleaning our house.

All this was beyond overwhelming for someone not used to being on the receiving end. It was very uncomfortable for me to have to be taken care of. I was confused and experienced mixed emotions. I was honestly grateful for all the help, but at the same time, almost embarrassed at being in a position of needing it. I was used to being the strong one, the person who gave the help. I remember when the Lord spoke to me that I needed to lay down my pride and learn to graciously receive. It was for a season, and my turn to reciprocate would come again. (I later joined a mother of multiples club and enjoyed being able to provide meals for expectant mothers, remembering what a blessing it was for me in our time of need.)

I will forever be grateful to our family and friends who carried us those months until I was on my feet again. Especially do I honor my mother-in-law, Grandma Eileen, who devoted her help full time those first months when all three were in diapers. Her assistance (as well as Grandma Dotty's) was especially necessary because for insurance reasons I needed to work!

As far as the twins, by God's grace and much prayer, the experts were wrong – all except the dear geneticist who told me, "You could just be carrying two very different babies, genetically speaking." Sure enough, that is exactly what was happening. Both my son and daughter were born healthy and strong and came home immediately with me from the hospital. To this day they continue to have very different builds, much to the relief of my daughter, as she is the smaller one!

A lot happened during the first year and a half with three babies plus a demanding job. I learned that working part-time managing two levels of staff (24x7) was not practical while also trying to raise three babies. I learned that nursing multiple babies is very taxing on the body. I learned that if I didn't take care of myself by getting enough sleep, proper nutrition, etc., my body would start to give out. Simply put – I was trying to be everything for everyone, and it wasn't working very well. I was off balance and something had to change.

Fortunately, my husband earns a good income (and our insurance situation changed), which allowed us to make the decision for me to stay at home. For some readers, this would seem like a fantastic option. For me, someone who had not babysat as a teenager (except for my youngest sister), who had built up a solid career (I made VP before 30), and who never saw herself as a stay-at-home mom, it was an overwhelming decision. I didn't mind so much losing almost half our income, though this was certainly an adjustment! It was more about what was happening with my friendship circle. I felt caught in the middle between those who felt I had betrayed the working women's cause by staying at home, and those who felt it was the only answer. Then there was the loneliness that crept in due to spending most of my waking hours with three babies, and the monotony of changing diapers all day long. I still remember as if it were yesterday when I started introducing the twins to finger food. Kai thought it would be so funny to show the twins how to have a food fight! Spaghetti and mandarin oranges were on the walls, in their hair, on the floor, just everywhere. I cried as I took all three out of their respective high chairs and put them down where we played on the living room floor till daddy came home and could help clean up.

It was during this time when I was barely holding on, that I wondered if any of this was even worth it. Gone were the daily devotions. I was lucky to get a shower every day. Gone was my sense of control. I felt guilty about everything. I felt I was failing everyone. I remember talking with my mom who shared something a good friend of hers, Diane Sloan, had said concerning her time home with young ones: "Some days all you can do is thank God you are saved." So simple yet so profound; this was such a relief to me – here was a powerful woman of God, someone I respected, one of my mom's peers, and what she said was so easy! I had to understand and embrace the season of life in which I was.

At that point in my life, even though I had known and walked with the Lord for many years, the best I could do was latch on to a famous Scripture and thank God on a daily basis that I was saved.

*For God so loved the world that He gave His
only begotten Son, that whoever believes in
Him shall not perish, but have eternal life.*
John 3:16 NIV

However, this was okay. I know I didn't handle everything the best way — what God was teaching me through
those early years of my children's lives could fill multiple
chapters, but for now suffice it to say that God never gives
you more than you can handle. He always has a purpose
and a plan. God needed to hit me over the head so-to-
speak with three babies in order to teach me about dying
to self, putting aside my needs and desires, and to be
faithful in the little things that no one else saw or cared
about. I needed to learn that He wasn't up there marking
off a big checklist about how many times I prayed that
day or if I had my devotion time. Yes, these things are
important and absolutely essential, but sometimes God
just wants us to rest in the knowledge that He loves and
cares for us.

She looks well to the ways of her household. . . .
Proverbs 31:27 NASB

Most of us are well acquainted with Proverbs 31. I've
had the pleasure and benefit of hearing my mom share
on this Scripture many times. I especially appreciate her
humor, questioning what exactly the husband was doing
while the wife was so busy, but I digress!

Let's move forward a few years, all three were potty
trained now and feeding themselves reasonably well. The
house was still a wreck by my standards (I am my father's

daughter, you see – with an extremely type A person-ality!) but my children were happy and my husband con-tent. Yet, where was I in all this? I was spending too much of my time questioning my decision to stay at home. Was I sending the wrong message, especially to my daughter? How did I turn into this 50s "Leave it to Beaver" stereo-type? What about our retirement funds, etc.? I remember when the Lord clearly spoke to me that I had to make a choice, and either commit myself 100% to being a stay-at-home mom or make a change. Waffling was not the answer, and it was not honoring Him. My husband and I decided that I would continue to stay at home with the children. I determined to take Proverbs 31 to heart and do the best job I could, even if it was not so exciting or glamorous, and was actually pretty boring at times.

For me, these were the type of days when I had to dig deep and call upon the strength that the Lord (and my parents) had built into me. My prayer became, "I can do all things through Christ who strengthens me." I am strong in Christ Jesus, and I am more than a conqueror. Even if this is the 100th time I've cleaned up the floor this month, I'll do it again with a grateful heart. I filled our home with worship music, thanking the Lord for His mercy and good-ness – even when I didn't feel like it. It is easy to appear as if you are all spiritual and have it all together when worshipping Sunday morning, but what about when you are setting the table for the umpteenth time or washing laundry over and over again? We are instructed to do all things without murmuring and complaining. It is all about choices. Was I successful all the time? Absolutely not – but isn't that what sanctification is all about – the continued process of becoming more like Christ in our conduct and character?

We can look for opportunities in our current situations that we may otherwise not have. In my case, I learned there were working moms in the neighborhood whom I could help out when their child care fell through. I came to know different people on the playgrounds and at the "Mommy and Me" classes who I otherwise would not have. I was able to share in a low-key way about our God with people whose paths I otherwise would not have crossed. I decided to create a fun atmosphere in our home for my children's friends to feel welcome. And now, we are able to invite some of those same friends to youth service who may otherwise not have had the opportunity to hear about God.

We all have a sphere of influence – it may not initially be the sphere you would have chosen – but I encourage you to choose contentment wherever God has put you. Don't be half-hearted – this is not what God expects. Be faithful, and He will honor your faithfulness.

Some of you may be experiencing life with a complicated pregnancy, the joy of a newborn, the wonderful and challenging toddler years, working full-time outside the home, juggling a career and balancing home-life. Maybe this is all behind you, but someone younger can learn from your experience. Regardless of your current situation, or your current sphere of influence, God has you where you are for a purpose. What we choose to make of our situation is up to us. When it is all said and done may we all hear the words: "Well done, good and faithful servant" (Matthew 25:21). And, as my mom would say, don't forget to laugh!

Heavenly Father, help us each to honor You in whatever situation or season of life we find ourselves. Give us the strength and dignity, the depth of character, and the steadfastness to make the choices that bring You glory. In Your precious name we pray. Amen.

THE JOY OF DISCOVERY

Again, the kingdom of heaven is like treasure hidden in a field, which a man found and hid; and for joy over it he goes and sells all that he has and buys that field.
Matthew 13:44

*M*y conscious journey with the Lord began in March, 1951. However, as with all who have come to know and love Him, we soon learn that He began working in our lives long before we consciously yielded our hearts to Him. In fact, in the words of David, our Father God was always involved in our lives:

My frame was not hidden from You, when I was made in secret, and skillfully wrought in the lowest parts of the earth. Your eyes saw my substance, being yet unformed. And in Your book they all were written, the days fashioned for me, when as yet there were none of them.
Psalm 139:15-16

Once, while in the beautiful nation of Argentina, I experienced the deep joy of discovering yet another jewel of His beautiful nature. Charles and I accepted an invitation to go and experience the fresh winds of His Spirit moving in that hungry nation. While there, I became alarmingly ill with yet another skin infection. As I sat on the bed in the hotel, I began to weep with the discomfort and pain. Frustration gripped my heart about being in a foreign country battling an infection. Charles looked helplessly at me, and began to pray. All I could do was cry, "Lord, do You even see me – in the midst of this move of God, do you see what is happening to me?"

After a bit we made our way to the meeting room. The atmosphere was filled with praise and worship, but all I could do was quietly sit there and weep. I hurt both inside and out. In the midst of the worship a brother got up and began reading from Psalm 139. As he read from verse 16 (NIV): "Your eyes saw my unformed body," the voice of my beloved Shepherd came clearly into my heart, "My daughter, even while you were yet in your mother's womb, mine were the first eyes you looked into, I saw you then and see you now, for My eyes never stop watching over you, and looking into you."

Who can adequately explain such life-changing encounters? For in a moment of time, He removed from my heart the fear, frustration, and doubt, and gave to me His extraordinary Presence and peace. Once again His promise proved true:

He sent forth His Word and healed. . . .
Psalm 107:20

In an atmosphere of worship and revelation I experienced the joy of discovering, even as Hagar did, that we are in an intimate friendship with the God who sees:

> *Then she called the name of the LORD*
> *who spoke to her, You-Are-the-God-Who-Sees;*
> *for she said, "Have I also here seen Him who*
> *sees me?"*
> Genesis 16:13

No matter what our challenges or circumstances are, He not only hears our cry, but He sees us. He knows us by name, and nothing will ever separate us from His love and care. We can rest in the joy of who He is, and that He is a God who sees everything!

Father, You are a joy to know and to love. It's not always easy to trust You because sometimes Your ways are bewildering and confusing. But, thank You for always brooding over us and drawing us to bring us to a deeper revelation of joyfully discovering who You are, and that You are good and Your loving-kindness endures forever.

HEALING PEACE

A heart at peace gives life to the body. . . .
Proverbs 14:30a NIV

*"Peace I leave with you, My peace I give to you;
not as the world gives do I give to you. Let not
your heart be troubled, neither let it be afraid."*
John 14:27

The sun reflected off the ripples of the small lake and gave the appearance of dancing diamonds. The geese, ducks, and cranes cascaded on and off the lake as if each had an important mission to accomplish. As I sat in my chair quietly absorbing the beauty and peace of the scene before me, such incredible feelings of joy and gratitude filled my heart. Praise and thanksgiving freely flowed out of my mouth to my beloved Lord. His Presence was so real and precious at that moment, that I could only lift my hands to Him, and allow tears of gratitude to flow down my face. "Father I do delight to be Your daughter. I enjoy Your Presence more than anything else in my life. Great is Your faithfulness. Thank You for both the bitter and sweet times in our journey together."

Immediately the passage from Exodus 15 came to me with illumination and insight. Once again the Holy Spirit would be my Teacher and Counselor from the Word of God. The Israelites traveled in the desert for three days without water. When they finally found water they could not drink it because it was bitter. They called the place Marah or "bitter." As usual, their response was one of complaining and grumbling.

Even after the phenomenal, supernatural deliverance from the Egyptian pursuers, even after a time of praise and worship and prophetic dancing, even after such a victory over their enemy, they quickly forgot, and easily slipped back into a destructive pattern of negativity and grumbling. As I read these words, the Lord gently reminded me of my own negative, complaining tendencies. When testings, trials, and desert experiences come, I, too, have often failed the test.

As I sat in His Presence, a memory from a number of years ago came to mind. It was a very bitter and tumultuous season in our lives. I could find peace nowhere. Every time I felt as if I were getting some victory in the situation, something else would happen to bring even more upheaval and tension into our lives. I was exhausted from the battle. Never had I craved for peace and rest as I had then. We as a staff had gone away together for a short period of time, trying to pray and gain perspective on all that was occurring. While there, even more "stuff" began happening. With tears in my eyes, I remember looking at our daughter, Dianna, and saying that I longed for peace. Lord, when will I find some peace? Later that day, Dianna came with a banner that she had just purchased for me from the book store. "Mom, this is the Word of the Lord for you." As I unfolded the beautiful banner I read:

The work of righteousness will be peace,
and the effect of righteousness, quietness and
assurance forever.
Isaiah 32:17

My people will dwell in a peaceful
habitation, in secure dwellings,
and in quiet resting places. . . .
Isaiah 32:18

This rhema word of the Lord pierced my heart, and for the first time in weeks I actually heard His voice: "I promise you peace and rest, but now you must use every spiritual weapon I have given you to win this battle." During the next weeks the weapons of forgiveness, praise, faith, the Word of God, prayer, and laughter would only trickle out of me. Inside I felt dry, wounded, and almost lifeless, but I knew Him better than that. So, I once again chose to let the river of praise and forgiveness not to simply trickle, but to flow. It took time and determination, but after a while, the break-through started to happen.

I remember ministering in Pennsylvania during that painful season, when my friend and fellow minister, Mary Ann Brown, looked at me as she was speaking. She then walked down the platform and gave a pointed, clear, and specific Word over my life. It was so direct and specific to my present situation that one of the women from Immanuel's who was sitting behind me began to cry along with me. Essentially the Word from the Lord was that this trial would not bring me defeat, but was going to be used of the Lord to bring us into a wide place. The best was yet to come! Hope and renewed faith filled my heart.

He also brought me out into a broad place;
He delivered me because He delighted in me.
Psalm 18:19

In the midst of this painful experience my beloved Mom went into the Presence of the Lord. The pain of her loss to us as a family was keenly felt. Even though the Lord had given me precious Words of promise, I still needed to walk by faith through this "valley of the shadow of death."

There were many accumulated losses during that season of my life. Yet, pain and loss have an amazing way of driving us into the arms of the Father of all comfort, of taking us to deeper places in the fellowship of His suffering, and of sharpening our spiritual vision and perspective. I knew I needed to allow suffering to do its work of deeper intimacy with Him.

Mom, who had always blessed me in her life, now in her death had also left my brother and me a small, hard-earned inheritance. Years before I remember walking along the beach in Ocean City, Maryland. I stopped and refreshed my soul by just watching the majesty of the waves breaking onto the shore. Since it was early morning, not too many folks were there. When I again began to walk the beach, I experienced the delight of His Presence. As I shared my heart and thoughts with my best Friend, I remember stopping and saying, "You know, Lord, I feel almost guilty asking this, but I sure would enjoy having a place down here by the ocean." I then remember laughing because in the natural this was most unlikely.

I forgot about this conversation until about fifteen years later. Charles and I felt His nudging to use Mom's small inheritance towards a family beach house. Never will I forget walking into a small but appealing townhouse overlooking a lovely little lake, two miles from the beach. I felt the Lord's Presence surround me. I could almost see His smile and wink as these words filled my heart, "Here is the place we talked about fifteen years ago. It is for you, a place of peace and rest."

Delight yourself also in the LORD, and He shall
give you the desires of your heart.
Psalm 37:4

So I now sat in our house of peace, enjoying His Presence and His Word. As I continued to meditate on Exodus 15:22-27, I realized that in every desert experience we need to learn the power of the cross to change our grumbling into gratitude, and our whining into worship. Into this challenging Exodus account came a new revelation of the Lord's nature and desire towards us. He is our Healer!

"If you diligently heed the voice of the LORD
your God and do what is right in His sight, give
ear to His commandments and keep all His
statutes, I will put none of the diseases on you
which I have brought on the Egyptians. For I am
the LORD who heals you."
Exodus 15:26

My eyes and heart were then riveted on Exodus 15:27:

Then they came to Elim, where there were
twelve wells of water and seventy palm trees;
so they camped there by the waters.

As I meditated on these verses I heard His still small voice: "My daughter, throughout your life's journey, I have led you through your valleys and deserts, but I will always bring you to Elim, a place of nourishment and refreshment. Here I allow you to "camp" and remain for a season. After the battles, enjoy your season of peace and rest." Elim means "large trees, a place of strong, tall palm trees" – a place of beauty, rest, and peace!

Such awe filled my heart. As I continued to allow the beauty and peace of His Presence to wash over me, I realized that the seasons of refreshment were indeed great and more frequent than were the desert seasons of tears and grief. Hallelujah, what a Savior!

You are awesome, majestic, and absolutely delightful! Thank You, thank You, for the sheer joy of being Your Daughter! Thank You for Your healing gift of peace and rest in every season of our lives!

WATER WALKERS

I can do all things through
Christ who strengthens me.
Philippians 4:13

*I*t was our regular Wednesday staff worship and fellowship time. As we sat around the tables listening to our
young missionaries share their hearts, I experienced the
stirring of the Holy Spirit within me.

Two precious young people had met one another while
counseling at our Camp Sonshine, held at Immanuel's each
summer. We watched their relationship grow and soon
they were married. Almost immediately they answered
the call to serve the Lord in the Philippines. A small group
of young people went off to minister to the orphans and
discarded children in an area outside of Manila. As they
shared about the desperate needs of these children, tears
ran down their faces. On one occasion this small group of
missionaries scattered themselves among the needy children, talking with them, feeding them, and speaking to
them of a new life of hope in Jesus. Jesse recounted that
when they all returned to their small apartment to give

their progress reports, they realized that they had each said "yes" to the children's specific requests. They were a little dismayed as to what they all had committed themselves. It then dawned on them what they had called their ministry, *Walk on Water*. They embraced this challenge, and with tears running down their faces shared how God continued to meet their needs and the desperate needs of the children.

As they continued to share the passion and zeal of their young hearts, I too began to weep. I felt His Spirit moving upon me and heard: "You used to be like that, My daughter. You were very zealous, and willing to take risks for Me."

My mind went back to the many times we jumped out of the boat in our zeal for Him. We went into the restaurant business, bought an apartment house, and owned two campgrounds. We opened one campground free of charge to hundreds of people during the "Jesus People" movement. We fed them and housed them, served and ministered to them, and all because we felt we heard His voice. Looking back upon our lives I realized we too had been "Water Walkers," willing to risk getting out of the boat of our own comfort and safety zone. In that moment of encounter with the Lord, I also realized that I had become much more conservative and "discerning" in how I now lived. To His probing statement: "You used to be like that," I finally responded, "Yes, Lord, but there were times when I felt like You let me sink, and I wasn't so ready to jump out of the boat again. In fact, Lord, risk-taking isn't as desirable now as it was when I was younger." Sitting at that table, I became enveloped in the arms of His love and

His understanding. He didn't condemn me, but His goodness did lead me to repentance.

From the depths of my heart I asked Him to restore to
me that radical, risk-taking, passionate obedience of first
love. "Lord, let me be a Holy Ghost Water Walker in this
later season of my life."

It never ceases to amaze me how Jesus can take us
into the secret places of His heart even in public places.
I doubt whether anyone that day even recognized that I
was having a life-changing encounter with the Captain of
the ship of my life, but when I returned to my office, He
and I had a more intimate relationship than I had when
the day began. I didn't know what it all would mean, but
a "Water Walker" I would be.

A couple of months had passed when I received an
invitation to speak and minister at a conference in Israel.
My dear husband and family almost immediately dis-
missed the idea. The situation in Israel was in turmoil.
Suicide bombings and violent disturbances had erupted
all over the land. The State Department had issued strong
travel warnings, and the newspapers were daily reporting
on the turbulent events over there. Tourism was virtually
down to nothing, and hotels and restaurants were empty,
and many were closed. Out of love and concern for me,
my family and friends counseled me to wait to go at a
more peaceful time (which for Israel seems to be rare).

I soberly held all their council before the Lord, but still
had no peace to write and say I would not come. One
morning, I laid the open letter on the kitchen counter.

"OK, Lord, You read this. What do You want me to do?"
"Its 'Water Walking' time, My daughter." I still smile at the
moment. Such a peace, joy, and assurance filled my heart
as I worshipfully said, "Yes, Lord." When I presented this to
Charles, he immediately said he would support my decision to go. He was concerned, but he knew I had heard His
voice. When I shared this with our Church family, immediately twelve women came to me and said, "We're coming
with you," to which I emphatically responded: "No, you're
not. I barely have the faith for myself to go. I don't want
to have the responsibility for you as well." However, these
dear warrior women said they absolutely felt they were
to also go. Over the weeks they agreed to the following
stipulations. They could not bring personal problems with
them. They had to raise not only all their own funds, but
also enough to leave for the Messianic believers. Also,
they had to be willing to work in whatever capacity they
were needed without grumbling, to make this conference
a success. After much prayer and discussion all 12 women
came with me to Israel.

We found our hearts knit in strong ties of love and
compassion for our brothers and sisters in the land. Our
concerns for safety seemed so insignificant in the realiza-
tion that our Messianic brothers and sisters always lived
in this culture of turmoil, fear, and uncertainty. For all of
us who went, our lives were forever changed. Vividly I
remember embracing both Arab and Jewish women, and
thanking God for having a small part in this restoration of
His people to Himself in the land of Israel. I realized He
is indeed raising up an army of "Water Walkers" from all
over the earth.

Thank You, Lord, that we are able to be part of Your amazing end-time purposes, and help us to boldly leap out into Your purposes, hearing Your Word:

> *But immediately Jesus spoke to them, saying,*
> *"Be of good cheer! It is I; do not be afraid."*
> Matthew 14:27

Impart to us Your faith to become radical, passionate, obedient Water Walkers.

THE LEAP OF JOY

. . .whom having not seen you love.
Though now you do not see Him,
yet believing, you rejoice with joy
inexpressible and full of glory. . . .
1 Peter 1:8

J oy, laughter, and healing are some of my favorite subjects to think and to teach about. Whenever I am studying the Scripture, I'm always alert to the word "joy." For example, there is something about each of us that gives God great joy:

The LORD your God in your midst, the Mighty
One, will save; He will rejoice over you with
gladness, He will quiet you with His love, He
will rejoice over you with singing.
Zephaniah 3:17

The word "rejoice" used in this Scripture is "exult," which actually means to bounce up and down like a ball. When we respond to His love, our God actually dances with joy over us. He enjoys us and delights in us! John 15:9-11 (NIV) gives us another insight into the joy of God:

"As the Father has loved me,
so have I loved you. Now remain in my love. If
you keep my commands, you will remain in my
love, just as I have kept my Father's commands
and remain in his love. I have told you this so
that my joy may be in you and that your joy
may be complete."

Even though Jesus is often referred to as a man of sorrow and familiar with suffering (Isaiah 53:3b), He is also a Savior filled with joy. In quoting from Psalm 45, the author of Hebrews writes of the Son:

"You have loved righteousness and hated
lawlessness; therefore God, Your God, has
anointed You with the oil of gladness more
than Your companions."
Hebrews 1:9

In John 15 Jesus tells us that as we live in and experience His transforming love for us, and as we lovingly obey Him, we will be filled with His overflowing joy. (His gift of joy is not only our strength, but also our source of creativity, energy, and health.) Proverbs 17:22a states that, "A cheerful heart is good medicine. . . ." Laugh, smile, God does love us unconditionally!

Recently I was drawn to meditate on a passage that repeatedly uses the words "joy" and "rejoicing." The context of this passage in Luke 10:17-21 is most illuminating. Jesus sent out 70 of His followers into the villages to preach the good news of the Kingdom. They returned filled with joy, and were rather amazed that, ". . .even the demons submit to us in Your name." Jesus was pleased, but adjusted their perspective on joy. The basis of rejoicing is not that we now have this kind of authority, but rather that our names are written in heaven. Joy, joy, joy, I have been redeemed by the blood of the Lamb! I am now a citizen of heaven! And for all eternity I will delight in His Presence and love.

What happened next was a delightful insight into the captivating nature of Jesus. In that hour Jesus *rejoiced* in the Spirit and said,

> *"I thank You, Father, Lord of heaven*
> *and earth, that You have hidden these things*
> *from the wise and prudent and revealed them*
> *to babes. Even so, Father, for so it seemed good*
> *in Your sight."*
> Luke 10:21

Just picture this scene. The disciples' success in bringing healing and deliverance to others through the preaching of the Gospel so filled Jesus with joy and rejoicing that He could not keep from dancing. One translation for the phrase "full of joy" is "much jumping." I see Jesus leaping and jumping before His Father and, in my paraphrase, saying: "Yippee, Daddy, they are actually getting my message. Thank you, Father, for bringing revelation to them of who I am, and who they are because of Me!" As I pondered these profound statements, I sensed Him saying, "Yes, My child, whenever you're about My business, moving in the revelation of who I am, and the authority I've given you, you cause Me to rejoice over you with dancing and your joy becomes full."

Thank You, Lord, for Your gift of joy and for the work of Your Spirit who imparts it to us. Let Your joy flow through us, bringing salvation and healing to all we encounter. Thank You for the truth of Psalm 16:11:

You will show me the path of life; in Your presence is fullness of joy; at Your right hand are pleasures forevermore.

JUICY WITH AGE

*The righteous shall flourish like a palm tree,
he shall grow like a cedar in Lebanon. Those
who are planted in the house of the LORD shall
flourish in the courts of our God. They shall still
bear fruit in old age; they shall be fresh and
flourishing, to declare that the LORD is upright;
He is my rock, and there is no unrighteousness
in Him.*
Psalm 92:12-15

What an inspiring, thought-provoking Psalm. For years I have pondered the depth of meaning found in these words. It's obvious the Lord has much to teach us from His creation of trees. The righteous, those who love God, are destined to thrive, prosper, and flourish in Him. The psalmist compares the believer to a palm tree. In studying the palm tree we find that it's created to withstand storms. It is often blown virtually to the ground, but the resilient flow of life within causes it to rebound, and stabilize. It is also noted that the older the tree gets, the juicier its fruit is! The righteous also grow like the cedar tree. Strong, sturdy, and stately were the cedars of Lebanon – often used to build majestic structures. I still smile as I remember the yearly ritual during my youth, of Mom putting all the woolens into the cedar closet each spring. The fragrance of cedar would protect from insects and moths (cedar repels pests).

The righteous allow themselves to be planted in the house of the Lord. In these tumultuous days it is critical that He plants us among His people, for there, in the place He has prepared for us, we will flourish and blossom with fruit. Then the promise is given that as we grow older, we will still remain fruitful, staying fresh and green. These words bring to mind a plump, juicy peach. For believers, our destiny includes becoming more juicy and delightful with age. Not too long ago I was captured by David's statement in Psalm 71:17,18:

O God, You have taught me from my youth;
and to this day I declare Your wondrous works.
Now also when I am old and gray headed,
O God, do not forsake me, until I declare Your
strength to this generation, Your power to
everyone who is to come.

I read these words back to the Lord, and smiled. The words were like a fire in my heart. I sensed His Presence as I renewed my commitment to Him to continue to serve His purposes, not only in my generation, but also in the next generation as well. As I sat before Him, I repeated the prayer of the Psalmist to ". . .declare His power to the next generation."

I felt Him say, "Can you embrace the call of Caleb for your generation?" Quickly I read and reread the wonderful words found in Joshua 14:6-14:

> Then the children of Judah came to Joshua in
> Gilgal. And Caleb the son of Jephunneh the
> Kenizzite said to him: "You know the word
> which the LORD said to Moses the man of God
> concerning you and me in Kadesh Barnea. I was
> forty years old when Moses the servant of the
> LORD sent me from Kadesh Barnea to spy out
> the land, and I brought back word to him as
> it was in my heart. Nevertheless my brethren
> who went up with me made the heart of the
> people melt, but I wholly followed the LORD
> my God. So Moses swore on that day, saying,
> 'Surely the land where your foot has trodden
> shall be your inheritance and your children's
> forever, because you have wholly followed the
> LORD my God.' And now, behold, the LORD has
> kept me alive, as He said, these forty-five years,
> ever since the LORD spoke this word to Moses
> while Israel wandered in the wilderness; and
> now, here I am this day, eighty-five years old.
> As yet I am as strong this day as on the day
> that Moses sent me; just as my strength was
> then, so now is my strength for war, both for
> going out and for coming in. Now therefore,
> give me this mountain of which the LORD spoke
> in that day; for you heard in that day how the
> Anakim were there, and that the cities were
> great and fortified. It may be that the LORD will
> be with me, and I shall be able to drive them

out as the LORD said." And Joshua blessed
him, and gave Hebron to Caleb the son of
Jephunneh as an inheritance. Hebron therefore
became the inheritance of Caleb the son of
Jephunneh the Kenizzite to this day, because he
wholly followed the LORD God of Israel.

Prophetically, I sensed the Lord desires to stir up a whole older generation who often feel they've missed God, who lament that they are too old, or feel it's simply too late to fulfill their God-given destinies. At age 85 Caleb knew there were still mountains to conquer and land to possess.

Imagine waiting 40 years to fulfill your destiny. I often wonder what those years were like for Caleb. After all, it wasn't his fault that he was stuck in this wilderness. He had the faith in God 40 years earlier to conquer the land, but the unbelief and stubbornness of those around him caused him to have to wait for 40 long, tedious years. I wonder if he ever struggled with anger and issues of unforgiveness, bitterness, and resentment against his rebellious brethren. If Caleb had these struggles, it is obvious that he had to have gained the victory. For even now he could boldly come to Joshua and declare, "It is time!"

The words Caleb used in Joshua 14:11 (NIV) are most inspiring:

"I am still as strong today as the day Moses
sent me out; I'm just as vigorous to go out to
battle now as I was then."

Pondering these words makes me want to shout to the maturing generation: "Wake up, arise, be strong in His strength and joy. You have much land to yet possess!" There is a whole new generation of children and grand-children to fight for and see released into their ordained destinies.

Charles and I were birthed in a season of revival, and have been privileged to be a part of every fresh move of His Spirit since we began our journey in the early 50s. When you experience the river of the Holy Spirit in revival dynamic, you are never again the same. During these years we have often said to one another: "Do you smell the rain coming?" As in the natural, so it is in the Spirit, the rains of revival are on the horizon, and the great harvest is already beginning. Laborers from every generation are now being called to arise:

> *Arise, shine; for your light has come! And the*
> *glory of the LORD is risen upon you. for behold,*
> *the darkness shall cover the earth, and deep*
> *darkness the people; but the LORD will arise*
> *over you, and His glory will be seen upon you.*
> Isaiah 60:1,2

Regardless of age, gender, or culture, those of us who know and love the Lord are being called to "Arise and shine!" Every time I read Peter's bold proclamation in Acts 2:17,18, something leaps in my spirit. "Your old men will dream dreams," and all will prophesy the word of the Lord in these last days. There is a younger generation longing to hear from their spiritual mothers and fathers. There is a yearning for encouragement, not criticism, for fire and not smoldering ashes. A desire to hear how we have walked, dreamed, and repeatedly proven His faithfulness is coming from the younger believers.

Never will I forget an experience Charles and I had as we were ministering out west. Most of the folks were precious older saints, many of whom had come out of past, powerful revivals. Now they sat mostly in the back, some with their arms crossed, some looking even bored. Suddenly the back doors opened, and in came a group of young people ranging in age from 18 to 22 years. They came to the front and almost immediately joined in the flow of worship with shouting, leaping, and dancing. The contrast between the generations would have made me laugh, if it hadn't been so sad. The Scripture from Matthew 9:17 came to mind:

"Nor do they put new wine into
old wineskins, or else the wineskins break,
the wine is spilled, and the wineskins are
ruined. But they put new wine into new
wineskins, and both are preserved."

As I sat there I cried out to the Lord, "Keep me from becoming a dried up old wineskin unable to receive the new wine of Your Spirit."

When Charles and I were introduced as the morning speakers, I could see the disappointment come over the faces of the young people. I knew they wondered if they would once again be disappointed in hearing only about what God had done in years past. The hunger in their young hearts to hear a fresh, new word from God touched me deeply. As I yielded to the fire of His Spirit within me, I heard a fresh prophetic word virtually erupt from inside of me. It turned out to be quite a morning; even some of the older generation seemed to catch the fire again.

Later on, as I was combing my hair in the restroom, one of the young leaders approached me. She hesitated, and then blurted out, "You surprised me. When you got up to speak, I truthfully wondered if someone as. . . ." She looked a little embarrassed, and so I helped her out. I put my arm around her and smiled. "I know, you wondered if someone as old as me really had something to say to your generation." I gave her a squeeze and laughed. "You know there are many of us who still carry the fire and the zeal to proclaim His wonders to the next generation." As we stood there in the ladies restroom, she sadly confessed that they were a group of youth who had been sent to minister to many different groups, and that mostly they found the older folks to be critical of how they looked and how they worshipped. They often left these gatherings more discouraged than when they first went in. Right there in the restroom we held hands and prayed that the Lord would change this situation. We asked for an inter-generational anointing that would cause all, young, old, and middle aged to link arms for the kingdom purposes, to stand together to win a lost world to Himself, and to help usher in the coming of the King.

Do these aches, pains, and at times serious physical issues accompany the aging process? Absolutely! I cared for four of my aging family members and for twelve years was a first-hand observer of these challenges. But, I also saw the power of love, joy, and laughter in keeping family members productive and active. At 88 my mother-in-law was part of our clowning ministry at church, which included hospital visitation and weekly visits to the elderly in nursing homes! Frequently I have pondered Paul's words:

Therefore we do not lose heart. Even though
our outward man is perishing, yet the inward
man is being renewed day by day.
II Corinthians 4:16

God's heart and purpose for us is that inside, where the fruit of the Spirit is cultivated, we will always remain "fresh and green" and juicy with life! And the rich life of Christ within will also overflow to give strength and energy to what is outside – our physical bodies.

Even the youths shall faint and be weary, and
the young men shall utterly fall, but those who
wait on the Lord shall renew their strength;
they shall mount up with wings like eagles,
they shall run and not be weary, they
shall walk and not faint.
Isaiah 40:30-31

Thank You, Lord, for Caleb's example of courage and determination to take the "hill country," along with the next generation. Keep our wine-skins soft, flexible, and pliable so that we may always receive the new wine of Your Spirit. And give us, Lord, a powerful intergenerational anointing for these last days.

WILL HE FIND FAITH?

*But without faith it is impossible to please Him,
for he who comes to God must believe that
He is, and that He is a rewarder of those who
diligently seek Him.*
Hebrews 11:6

*I*n the midst of a deep sleep, I suddenly awoke with a phrase running through my mind, "When the Son of Man returns, will He find faith on the earth?" Over and over again I repeated the phrase in my mind. As I meditated on each word, I found I didn't even know the context. In order to fully understand this Scripture the context in which the words were spoken was essential. Finally I fell asleep again, questioning what kind of faith Jesus was looking for upon His return. The next morning I found the Scripture in its surprising context:

> *Then He spoke a parable to them,
> that men always ought to pray and not lose
> heart, saying: "There was in a certain city a
> judge who did not fear God nor regard man.
> Now there was a widow in that city; and she*

came to him, saying, 'Get justice for me from
my adversary.' And he would not for a while;
but afterward he said within himself, 'Though
I do not fear God nor regard man, yet because
this widow troubles me I will avenge her, lest
by her continual coming she weary me.'" Then
the Lord said, "Hear what the unjust judge
said. And shall God not avenge His own elect
who cry out day and night to Him, though He
bears long with them? I tell you that He will
avenge them speedily. Nevertheless, when the
Son of Man comes, will He really find faith on
the earth?"
Luke 18:1-8

It was a parable on prayer in which Jesus was teaching that His followers ". . .should always pray and never give up." Now, the subject of prayer has always left me with many unanswered questions. And I am apparently not alone, if one judges by the number of people who actually consistently respond to the call of prayer. In fact many prayer meetings have been rather boring and tedious to me. Everyone seemed to be praying his own agenda, and then we seemed to give the Lord our opinions as to how all these issues of concern should be answered. Often I have left prayer times rather confused and feeling there had to be more to this call to prayer than many of us were experiencing.

In this passage Jesus told us that we are always to pray, and never give up. He then gave us a parable of a widow woman, who demonstrated such tenacity, perseverance, and persistence in her request for justice from a godless judge, that he finally gave her what she asked for. In fact she made quite a pest of herself: ". . .the widow keeps bothering me." Then Jesus piercingly drives home His point:

Then the Lord said, "Hear what
the unjust judge said. And shall God not
avenge His own elect who cry out day and
night to Him, though He bears long with them?
I tell you that He will avenge them speedily.
Nevertheless, when the Son of Man comes,
will He find faith on the earth?"
Luke 18:6-8

What a window into the subject of prayer from the perspective of Jesus! Obviously, when He returns the persevering and persistent prayers of His people will demonstrate a faith in Him that He yearns to see us exemplify. Luke 11:13 teaches us not only "The Lords' Prayer," but also about the boldness and persistence that He is looking for.

A number of months ago as I was in my morning "prayer time," I realized my mind was wandering all over, and that I was actually motivated by wanting to fulfill my religious commitment to a daily "quite time." Finally I just stopped, and looked up and said "Lord, are you as bored with my prayers as I am?" Immediately, the statement, "Yes, I am," flashed across my mind. "Well Lord, if prayer is so crucial, I ask you, as did your disciples, to teach me to pray."

I reread numbers of books on prayer and diligently searched the Scriptures on the subject. Most of the biblical heroes of faith simply talked to Him as the overflow of a shared life of fellowship and friendship. Moses stood out as a powerful man of intercession.

Exodus 33:11 tells us that the Lord spoke to Moses face to face as a man speaks with his friend. Abraham, David, Daniel, the prophets of old, as well as the heroes of the New Testament all give testimony to the power of prayer coming quite naturally from an intimacy of relationship between friends.

It soon became clear to me that the most essential ingredient for a fruitful prayer life is spending time with the Lover of our souls. Establishing a time and place for a period of deep silence and for the cultivation of a listening ear is essential. This indeed becomes for us our secret place in God. From this "hiding place" we learn to know His heart, and to better hear His voice.

I recall a precious insight into this verse:

> *But He, because He continues forever, has an unchangeable priesthood. Therefore He is also able to save to the uttermost those who come to God through Him, since He always lives to make intercession for them.*
> Hebrews 7:24,25

As I thought about the power of Jesus always making intercession for us, I asked, "Lord, what are you praying about?" "If you are still enough you will enter into My prayers, for I desire for you to come into agreement with

Me." Immediately the Scripture from 1 John 5:14-15 came to mind:

*Now this is the confidence that we have in Him,
that if we ask anything according to His will,
He hears us. And if we know that He hears us,
whatever we ask, we know that we have the
petitions that we have asked of Him.*

With renewed expectation and growing faith, prayer is increasingly becoming as natural as breathing. The Scriptures on prayer are numerous, and they clearly invite us into a dynamic relationship with Him that moves both heaven and earth through our prayers and intercessions. Consider but a few of these Scriptures that invite us into a greater joy of discovering the adventures of prayer:

*Be anxious for nothing, but in everything by
prayer and supplication, with thanksgiving,
let your requests be made known to God;
and the peace of God, which surpasses all
understanding, will guard your hearts and
minds through Christ Jesus.*
Philippians 4: 6,7

*Confess your trespasses to one another, and
pray for one another, that you may be healed.
The effective, fervent prayer of a righteous man
avails much.*
James 5: 16

*If My people who are called by My name will
humble themselves, and pray and seek My*

face, and turn from their wicked ways, then I
will hear from heaven, and will forgive their sin
and heal their land.
2 Chronicles 7:14

Recently Charles and I prayed with a godly, very alert sister who is now 104 years old. She has been in our lives since we were 12 years old. As we left her room she said to us, "You know when I can't sleep, I pray around the world." What an example of faithfulness to God's call to pray regardless of age or circumstance! I will never forget her words on prayer.

Even though not all of my questions on prayer have been answered, I do have a fresh resolve that when He comes again, He will find in me an overflow of faith expressed in persistent, persevering, and passionate prayer.

Father, Thank You for the privilege of such a friendship, that together we can be world changers through the power of prayer. Indeed may we always pray and never give up.

THIRSTING FOR GOD

*As the deer pants for the water brooks, so
pants my soul for You, O God. My soul thirsts
for God, for the living God. When shall I come
and appear before God?*
Psalm 42:1,2

*T*here are precious times when I feel nestled in the
protective arms of the Father's love and compassion.
This usually occurs during the times that I become quiet
both on the outside and on the inside. Increasingly as His
child, I long for a quiet place and a quiet heart and mind.
As I make time to soak in His love and in His Word, my
longings for Him deepen and increase. And amazingly, I
discover His longing for time with me is even greater than
mine for Him!

Frequently I have pondered the dynamic of interaction
between the Lover and His beloved as found in Song of
Songs.

*"O my dove, in the clefts of the rock, in the
secret places of the cliff, let me see your face,*

*let me hear your voice; for your voice is sweet,
and your face is lovely."*
Song of Songs 2:14

It is as the beloved sequesters herself in the cleft of the rock, and in the secret hiding place, that she hears the voice of the Lover of her soul: ". . .show me your face, let me hear your voice." To Him our voice of love and worship is sweet, and our uplifted, transparent face is lovely. Jesus is our Rock, our Fortress, our Deliverer, our Strong Tower, our Shield, our Refuge and our Strength, and our Lover, a very present help in the time of trouble. The cleft in the rock speaks to us of Jesus' death on the cross. When we hide ourselves in the wounds of Jesus, we experience His love, forgiveness, cleansing, and mercy in ever deeper ways. As we learn to abide in the secret place of His love and yearning for us, something within us begins to cry out for holiness, purity, and a deep heart transformation. In light of such love and longing that proceeds from the Lover of her soul, the beloved one cries out:

*Catch us the foxes, the little foxes that spoil the
vines, for our vines have tender grapes.*
Song of Songs 2:15

What are these little foxes that ruin the fruitfulness of our lives? As I was pondering this, I realized that I actually enjoyed watching the little foxes. They were so cute, and seemed so little and innocent. It was then that I heard His voice. "It is not only the huge and obvious sins that steal your fruitfulness, but also those little sins of the mind, the mouth, and especially of the heart. It is only in the hiding place of My love that I reveal those things in your life that grieve My Presence and quench the fire of My Spirit from burning brightly within you."

Charles and I were birthed into the Kingdom in the early 50s during a season of revival. We were then privileged to be a part of every fresh move of the Spirit of God during the next 60 years. It is as if He marked us for deep moves of His Spirit during those encounters with Him over the years. We learned early that lukewarmness was not where we wanted to live.

> *"I know your works, that you are neither cold*
> *nor hot. I could wish you were cold or hot. So*
> *then, because you are lukewarm, and neither*
> *cold nor hot, I will vomit you out of My mouth."*
> Revelation 3:15,16

The longer we walk with the Lord, the hungrier we become for more of His Presence and power in our lives. It became very apparent to us that regardless of what was happening around us, we could always live in *personal* revival. The Song of Songs opens to us the beauty of an intimate, revelatory relationship with our beloved Lord. Repeatedly our Lover beckons and invites us to Himself.

> *My beloved spoke, and said to me: "Rise up, my*
> *love, my fair one, and come away."*
> Song of Songs 2:10

As we are drawn more deeply into the secret places of His heart, and into an experience of personal revival, we hear Him speak to us of the "little foxes" in our lives. He loves us too much to allow us to continue with hidden "joy and revival killers" in our lives. David prayed a powerful prayer for inner cleansing and exposure of His heart.

Search me, O God, and know my heart;
try me, and know my anxieties; and see if there
is any wicked way in me, and lead me in the
way everlasting.
Psalm 139:23,24

So in our quests for personal revival and intimacy with Him must we also invite Him into all of the hidden places of woundedness, sin, and disobedience. This journey may take us to places of pride, self-centeredness, lust, greed, anger, laziness, unforgiveness, bitterness, or resentment. As we continue to hunger for His Presence in our lives, the revelation of His holiness and purity will continue to expose any and all areas of darkness or brokenness within us. Isaiah experienced eternal, inner change as he beheld the glory of the holiness of the Lord.

"Holy, holy, holy is the LORD of hosts;
the whole earth is full of His glory!"
Isaiah 6:3b

As he saw the exaltedness of Jehovah, Isaiah was immediately led to a place of repentance, cleansing, and of sending into the purposes of God. Anyone who continues to hunger and thirst after God will often have an "Isaiah 6" experience. All genuine revival, both personal and corporate, will always usher us into a greater experience of repentance, transformation, and intimacy with our beloved Lord Jesus.

A great awakening is beginning to unfold around the earth. Seasons of intense prayer, worship, and evangelism are flowing from these fresh rivers of revival. The Lord's beautiful Bride, composed of both Jew and Gentile, is making herself ready for the beloved Bridegroom. In the language of the Song of Songs, the Bride is joyously proclaiming:

"I belong to my Lover, and His desire is for me."
Song of Songs 7:10

In this experience of being unconditionally loved and accepted in the Beloved, the Bride yearns to be made completely whole, pure and holy for her Bridegroom. A number of years ago, as I spent many weeks studying and meditating on our tremendous Lover as He is revealed to us in the Song of Songs, I was especially impacted by one verse:

Who is this coming up from the wilderness, leaning upon her beloved? I awakened you under the apple tree. There your mother brought you forth; there she who bore you brought you forth.
Song of Songs 8:5

I made a study of the Word, "lean," and discovered that it also meant "trust." To trust is to lean on, and to place the weight of one's confidence on. I smiled as a picture came to my mind. Life is often like walking through many wilderness and desert experiences. But through it all, for those of us who truly thirst for our God, the "drier" our circumstances become, the harder we learn to lean upon the great Lover of our souls.

As I sat thanking my Lord and worshipping Him for always bringing us up and out of the deserts of life, I heard His whisper and saw a picture of Charles and myself. I saw us each heavily leaning upon each of His arms. As He was confidently walking, we were learning to lean even harder on His arms. Then I saw us a little battered and bruised from the journey, but we each had a smile of triumph on our faces, and I heard: "When your journey is completed, you will have weathered many storms, and many hard knocks, but as you learned to trust Me in every battle, as you learned to lean on My everlasting arms, I have brought you up from every desert experience into the wide places of My love, peace, and joy."

We will be glad and rejoice in you.
Song of Songs 1:4b AMP

Thank You, Lord, that our thirst for the water of life You offer us, is but a deep response to Your thirsting for us. You thirst for our love and our worship. Thank You that in Your eyes we are beautiful, lovely, and majestic. Continue to draw us, and we will run after You all the days of our lives!

IDENTITY THEFT
"WHO STOLE YOUR IDENTITY?"
By Jenny Schmitt Childers

*The thief does not come except to steal, and
to kill, and to destroy. I have come that they
may have life, and that they may have it more
abundantly.*
John 10:10

Several months ago, I was out on a date with my husband when the Lord suddenly spoke to me. I was in the bathroom of a movie theater washing my hands and looking into the mirror when the Lord spoke deep into my spirit, "Who stole your identity?" Gratefully, I was alone at the time, because that very simple question spoke so deeply into the core of my being that I began to cry. As I stood there in the bathroom still looking into the mirror, the Lord began to unfold the answer to the question He had just asked.

From as far back as I can remember, I have been called by a beloved family member a not so flattering nickname. Although it was meant as a term of endearment, as a small child, being called "Miss Piggy" negatively shaped who and what I thought of myself. As I stood in the bathroom of that movie theater, the Lord began to show me that my identity had been stolen by someone I loved. When you love someone, anything they give to you becomes a thing to be cherished. So I quickly began to cherish this false identity. As the Lord unfolded this truth to me, He explained that even though no child in their right mind would knowingly embrace being called a "piggy," those words dictated how I saw myself. In my mind, I was "Miss Piggy."

To cherish something means it's important to you. It's something you hold on to. If your house were on fire, and you had only a moment to grab one thing, most likely you would reach for something you cherished and could not live without. Often when you think of the word "cherish," it's in a positive way. But in this case, I want you to see how sometimes we can cherish things in an unhealthy way. For example, the words spoken over us, whether by a parent or an authority figure, often shape our world view and how we see ourselves. These words often become engrained in our spirit and soul in such a way that they form our identity and behavior.

Our identity is who we are. The word identification comes from the word identity. In today's world, we can't go anywhere without showing identification. If you want to drive a car, you need identification called a driver's license. If you want to travel, you need identification called a passport. If you want to buy a house or a car, you need to show identification proving that you are who you say you are. Identity and identification are important in the earthly realm, but even more important in the spiritual realm. Satan knows that you and I were made in the image of God. Genesis 1:27 says:

> *God created mankind in his own image, in*
> *the image of God he created them; male and*
> *female he created them.*

Our identity is that we are made in the image of God! Our personality is based on the image of God! Our talents are based on the image of God! Our intelligence is based on the image of God! If that identity is stolen from us at a young age, we spend the rest of our lives acting as if we have no idea who we are. When you don't know who you are, you can't walk in authority.

As the Lord continued to unfold the question, "Who stole your identity," He brought to my mind a little Scripture in the book of *Chronicles* called "The Prayer of Jabez."

> *Now Jabez was more honorable*
> *than his brothers, and his mother called his*
> *name Jabez, saying, "Because I bore him in*
> *pain." And Jabez called on the God of Israel*
> *saying, "Oh, that You would bless me indeed,*
> *and enlarge my territory, that Your hand would*
> *be with me, and that You would keep me*
> *from evil, that I may not cause pain!" So God*
> *granted him what he requested.*
> I Chronicles 4:9,10

We are not told the circumstances surrounding Jabez's birth, but Jabez's mother named her son in such a way that he walked through life knowing he caused his mother pain. From all the names his mother could have chosen, why did she chose Jabez? Did she understand the implications of labeling her child "the one I birthed in pain"? What a perfect example of how the enemy can use a situation to bring about the feeling of shame. Jabez would walk through life with everyone knowing he caused his mother pain. Jabez did not allow his mother's label to define his identity. The first thing the Bible tells us is that Jabez was more honorable than any of his other brothers! Instead of allowing shame and a label of "pain" to define his actions, his character and his destiny, Jabez was able to press into Almighty God and God renamed him "honorable."

When someone steals our God-given identity, it's often replaced with a cloak of shame. Like Jabez, many of us cannot outrun the psychological imprint of shame thrust upon us in our childhood. But wait, the story doesn't end there! I Chronicles chapter 4 goes on to say that Jabez cried out to God and asked God to bless him. Wow! Jabez was able to press past his shame, past his name, and tap into the saving love of God.

When you have a shame-based identity, you don't feel worthy of God's blessing. But when you step into your God-given identity, and your eyes are opened to the truth of who you really are, you begin to see yourself as a son or daughter of the Most High. As a child of God, of course you would feel comfortable going before your heavenly Father and asking Him to bless you; after all He's your Dad! Dads love to bless their kids!

Jabez was able to come into a clear understanding of his true identity and was able to stop the cycle of pain.

> *"Be with me, keep me from evil, that I may not cause pain!"*
> 1 Chronicles 4:10

When you are living apart from your God-given identity, you can't help but cause pain to those around you. There is a saying that goes, "Hurt people hurt people." When you are hurt, you hurt others. A person doesn't ask the Lord to keep them from hurting people unless they have a past history of causing pain.

A few years back, I was walking through a deep level of emotional turmoil and pain. Severely depressed and incredibly unhappy, I lashed out against one of my dearest friends and caused her tremendous pain. It's one of my biggest regrets in life. Not a week goes by that I don't feel the pain of losing that dear friend. I can totally understand why Jabez would ask the Lord to help him not to cause pain to others. The prayer of Jabez is such a short little prayer, it would be easy to look at it and immediately jump to the end where it says, "And God granted him what he requested." When I look at the prayer of Jabez, I see a prayer years in the making. I see a young man who had his identity stolen at birth. A false identity was given to him by his own mother. He spent years living with this false identity, probably in pain and causing others pain. However, Jabez had a God encounter that forever changed his life. God showed up and removed his false identity and reclothed him with a robe of righteousness. In God's eyes, Jabez was not a man who caused pain, he was a man who was more honorable than any of his brothers and God greatly blessed him.

Has your identity been stolen? I pray that today will be the start of your journey of knowing your true identity, and that you live in the authority of knowing who you are and why you were created. The Lord longs to talk with you, just as He spoke with me in the bathroom of that movie theater. He desires to give you the keys to true freedom so that you can live the blessed, fulfilled life that He has for you.

Lord, I am asking You to reveal to me any untruths that have shaped or formed my thinking in an ungodly way. Please reveal to me if my true God-given identity was stolen and replaced with a lie. Bring back to me any memories that need to be healed, so that You can speak truth into that situation, and set me free. I desire to live the life You have for me, and I want to be spiritually, emotionally, and physically healthy. I thank You that I can look at the prayer of Jabez and see that You are a God who loves to bless His children, and that no matter what was said or done to me as a child, You can set me free from that false identity and clothe me in a robe of righteousness.

SECURE, SIGNIFICANT, AND SANCTIFIED

*He is the image of the invisible God, the
firstborn over all creation. For by Him all things
were created that are in heaven and that are
on earth, visible and invisible, whether thrones
or dominions or principalities or powers. All
things were created through Him and for Him.
And He is before all things, and in Him all
things consist. And He is the head of the body,
the church, who is the beginning, the firstborn
from the dead, that in all things He may have
the preeminence.*
Colossians 1:15-18

One of the most profound and satisfying experiences of this earthly life is to immerse oneself in the beauty and magnificence of Jesus. To observe, study, and meditate on the unfolding revelation of Jesus in both the Old and New Testaments will always lead us to deeper places of worship, love, and adoration. No wonder all of heaven is filled with awe and wonder in the Presence of this One who is the "Word made flesh."

And the Word became flesh and
dwelt among us, and we beheld His glory, the
glory as of the only begotten of the Father, full
of grace and truth.
John 1:14

To recognize Jesus both as the Lamb of God who takes away the sins of the world, and to worship Him as the Lamb of God, who through His sacrifice on the cross has triumphed over sin, death, and evil, satisfies our hearts as nothing else in this world can. To be able to join in songs of praises, with all of heaven, brings to the human heart the deepest experience of fulfillment, peace, and joy that transcends all other joys.

Worthy is the Lamb who was slain to receive
power and riches and wisdom, and strength
and honor and glory and blessing!
Revelation 5:12

Still, how often is the exhilarating experience of worship interrupted by the everyday distractions and interactions. Frequently, I have told Charles that I think I would be perfect if it were not for other people! After an especially meaningful morning of prayer and study, I walked into the kitchen and found Charles rummaging through the refrigerator, "Did you forget to buy milk? And where are the eggs?" Having just come out of the "secret place," my very sanctified response was: "What, am I the only who shops around here?" As the "intense fellowship" increased between us, it quickly dawned on me that the revelation of the "secret place" had very obviously not yet translated to the transformation of the "inner place."

A groan escaped my lips as once again I saw the need of my own heart in contrast to some of the profound truths I was observing in the Scriptures. "Lord, help! I really want a pure heart and godly attitudes. Lord, You have worked so much grace into my life, and yet, I yearn for so much more. Lord, deliver me from selfishness, insecurities, and defensiveness." Even though Jesus was becoming more and more precious to me, I knew I still fell short of His desires for me to truly become like Him.

It was in the midst of one of these discouraging failures that I renewed my determination to learn more of Him. I let the beauty of His welcoming words wash over my hungry, inquiring soul:

"Come to Me, all you who labor and are heavy laden, and I will give you rest. Take My yoke upon you and learn from Me, for I am gentle and lowly in heart, and you will find rest for your souls. For My yoke is easy and My burden is light."
Matthew 11:28-30

Once again, the Holy Spirit was not only my Teacher, but also my Encourager assuring me of the truth of Paul's words:

. . .being confident of this very thing, that He who has begun a good work in you will complete it until the day of Jesus Christ. . . .
Philippians 1:6

Yes, He would finish the work, not only of justification, but also of sanctification deep within me. With renewed commitment to discover the keys of holiness in Jesus' life, I went back to serious study and meditation of His life in the Gospels. While I read and studied, I could actually feel His delight as I renewed my hunger for heart purity and holiness. Our Lord loves our pursuit of Him!

> *But without faith it is impossible to please Him,*
> *for he who comes to God must believe that*
> *He is, and that He is a rewarder of those who*
> *diligently seek Him.*
> Hebrews 11:6

One of the first Scriptures to be illumined to me with fresh insights on the depth of intimacy of relationship between Jesus and His Father is found in the words of Matthew 3:17:

> *And suddenly a voice came from heaven,*
> *saying, "This is My beloved Son, in whom I am*
> *well pleased."*

These words were spoken just to the Son. The Father knew how essential it was for Jesus to have His identity as His beloved Son firmly established. How He walked and talked flowed from this secure, intimate relationship. The Father spoke these powerful words of truth deep into the fabric of Jesus' life, and what they conveyed would establish the course of Jesus' earthly life and ministry. As I prayerfully read, reread, and chewed on each word, I began to understand how emotionally powerful they were. "This is My Son," conveys such a sense of belonging and of tender relationship between Father and Son. With the words, "whom I love," I believe Jesus experienced Himself wrapped in the arms of His Father's love, affection, and undivided attention. His Daddy was absolutely delighted in Him and found great joy in telling His Son of His love and tender affection.

"With Him, I am well pleased." These words spoke incredible validation, affirmation, and approval into Jesus' life. It appears obvious that thus far, Jesus had done no miracles, nor had He yet delivered His profound teachings. The Father loved His Son, not because of what He did, but because of who He was! The Father's love is unconditional.

As I let these powerful truths wash over me, I heard His quiet whisper, "And even so, do I love and delight in you. All holiness of heart springs from My unconditional love making your heart and mind whole. My Word promises to give health and healing and holiness into your life. Receive and enjoy My love." For the next moments I sat, basking in His love, acceptance, and tender affection. It was obvious that an essential key to Jesus' living in absolute purity and holiness resulted from the lavish love and delight the Father bestowed on Him. And so it is for us also!

> *The Lord your God in your midst, the Mighty*
> *One, will save; He will rejoice over you with*
> *gladness, He will quiet you with His love, He*
> *will rejoice over you with singing.*
> Zephaniah 3:17

In studying Matthew's Gospel, I saw that the account of Jesus' severe testing in the wilderness could not have been successfully completed without the Father's powerful validating of Jesus as His beloved Son. Satan challenged Jesus repeatedly about His identity: "If You are the Son of God. . . ." I am certain Jesus reflected back to the nurturing, life-giving words of the Father: "This is My Beloved Son. . . ." Jesus knew both the truth of the Scripture and had the experience of His Father's love encircling Him. This powerful combination of both Spirit and Truth is a transforming key in the hands of the Holy Spirit to bring us to inner wholeness and holiness.

Continuing my study into the secret of Jesus' humility and holiness, the words of John 13 arrested my attention: Again I read, and reread, asking the Holy Spirit for light:

> *Jesus, knowing that the Father had given all*
> *things into His hands, and that He had come*
> *from God and was going to God, rose from*
> *supper and laid aside His garments, took a*
> *towel and girded Himself.*
> John 13:3-4

Having had the privilege of knowing, loving, and serving Him from the early 1950's, Charles and I have gained much valued experience from observing many of His servants both fail and succeed in their walk with Him. Indeed, we ourselves have known deep seasons of failure, repentance, and restoration. I have sadly learned that the human heart is severely broken and bruised by sin and disobedience. It is almost shocking to watch pride, low self-esteem, anointing, insecurity, gifting, and manipulation at work within all of us, and often at the same time. The cry for reputation and respect are powerful driving forces in all of our lives. Often, unhealed leaders will attempt to dominate and control the sheep God has called them to tend and care for. The subtle lure of the praises and adulation of people has often led to tragic failure in the Kingdom of God.

In the context of John 13, as all the disciples were waiting to be served, and looking for someone else to wash their feet, Jesus Himself demonstrated the power of the Father's love. Jesus knew His identity and was secure as a Son when He got up and washed His disciples' feet. What a shock to the arrogance of the world systems that He who is greatest should become servant of all.

Jesus was absolutely secure in His Father's love, acceptance, and pleasure. Because He knew where He came from and where He was going, with genuine humility He could wash the feet of His disciples. Undoubtedly, they would often reflect back on their Master's words.

> *Now there was also a dispute among them,*
> *as to which of them should be considered the*
> *greatest. And He said to them, "The kings of*
> *the Gentiles exercise lordship over them, and*
> *those who exercise authority over them are*
> *called 'benefactors.' But not so among you; on*
> *the contrary, he who is greatest among you, let*
> *him be as the younger, and he who governs as*
> *he who serves."*
> Luke 22:24-26

As I once again basked in the illumination of these words, I felt a deep stirring in my soul. "The more transparent and honest you become before Me, the more you believe and receive My words of life, love, and affirmation; the more secure and joyful you will become. And you'll continue to learn that My greatest secrets are always revealed to those who humbly serve Me and My interests – especially in the lowly tasks." I then reflected on the fact that when Jesus turned the water into wine, only the servants knew how it happened. He still reveals His secrets to those who have learned how to humbly serve.

As I continue to study the beauty of Jesus' life and character, the more sensitive I seem to become to not wanting to grieve Him in my thoughts, attitudes, and words; the more I want to become like Him in purity and holiness. This is all the work of His grace!

It is essential to add one more practical implication for us in regard to our own personal interactions with our family and friends. In the raising of our children, both natural and spiritual, the words we speak and the environment we create with our very Presence is absolutely critical to raising healthy and whole children. To take time with them; to speak words of love, nurture, and acceptance to them; to validate who they are with words of appreciation and gratitude; to pray and proclaim their prophetic destiny in the Kingdom are essential ingredients to spiritual mentoring. Even when discipline and correction are required, it will come from a loving, redemptive heart and mouth. From our personal experience of being unconditionally loved, we will impart wholeness to others, especially to our families. (And remember to say, "forgive me, I was wrong," when we've blown it.)

Thank You, Lord, that You never allow us to abide in the secret place of revelation without working Your wholeness and holiness deep into the inner places of our hearts. Come, Holy Spirit, we welcome You to change us into the likeness of who You are.

> *And we know that all things work together for*
> *good to those who love God, to those who are*
> *the called according to His purpose.*
> *For whom He foreknew, He also predestined to*
> *be conformed to the image of His Son, that He*
> *might be the firstborn among many brethren.*
> Romans 8:28,29

HEARING HIS VOICE IN THE NATIONS

. . .Speak, Lord, for your servant is listening.
1 Samuel 3:9b NIV

*T*his was going to be a long trip for me! The suitcases were out, and once again I was sorting and arranging clothes to fit into one suitcase. What I packed had to suffice for about a month abroad. As I worked, I was praying and discussing the upcoming trip with the Lord. A small group of very faithful and fun women were traveling with me to minister in Scotland, Ireland, and then to Israel. In a most unique way the Lord had opened a door of favor in all three countries. There were people in these lands who had won a very special place of love and honor in my heart. I considered this month spent with them to be a very real privilege.

As I was packing and praying, I clearly heard the Lord say: "On this trip you are to listen more than you are to speak. I want you to learn from those to whom I send you. Be very sensitive to my Spirit, look, listen, and learn what I am doing in these nations." I sat down on the bed thinking again of Jesus' words: "He, who has ears, let him hear"

(Matthew 11:15). A Scripture in Proverbs 1:5 also caught my attention:

A wise man will hear and increase learning,
and a man of understanding will attain
wise counsel.
Proverbs 1:5

Even though I would have a rigorous schedule of teaching and ministering, I knew that this trip was primarily one in which I would be listening and learning from His Spirit and from His people in these different countries.

Charles and I have often reflected upon an unusual prophetic word we received when in our early thirties. We arrived late at a meeting in Springfield, Missouri, and as we walked in, the prophetic brother ministering, whom we had never met, called us up front. He told us he saw flags of many nations being waved over our heads. We were then living in a small town of 7,000 people in Northern Minnesota, and even though a love for the nations and especially for Israel, had always resonated in our hearts since we were teenagers, we didn't know how this vision to reach the nations for Christ would actually be worked out in us. Now we had this powerful word being spoken about us and the nations of the world. Afterwards Charles and I discussed this most pointed word about us and the nations, and wondered what it all meant practically.

Now here we are many years later, pastoring a precious and powerful congregation composed of more than 65 different nations. Virtually not a Sunday passes without us either receiving or sending folks into the nations. We have established a Bible School in India, and Charles recently traveled into eight different countries, teaching and training indigenous leaders. Sometimes I find myself almost stunned as to how beautifully God has fulfilled His prophetic word to us. Not only did He send us into the nations, but He strategically brought the nations to us!

As we were putting together last minute details for this trip, my excitement grew. I knew this trip was going to be life-changing for me. Increasingly my prayer was, "Lord give me a listening ear, and a tender, receptive heart to receive Your lessons for me from the nations."

Scotland is a beautiful, unique land, rich in history. Both the influence of the reformer John Knox, as well as the revival history of the Hebrides Islands off the West Coast of Scotland, had already made deep impressions on our lives. During the same period of history when Charles and I were converted to the Lord in the early 50s, the Holy Spirit fell on the islands of the Hebrides from about 1948-1954. This was a significant revival especially among the youth, and it was ushered in by two praying sisters in their 80's, and led by a godly preacher, Duncan Campbell. We found presently that there was a cry in the land of Scotland to once again redig the wells of revival waters.

As we were ministering, I found myself listening to different stories told by God's people. His grace amazed me profoundly as I listened to the many powerful testimonies of salvations, healings and deliverances. We had the privilege of staying in the Youth With A Mission base in Scotland. When we arrived we were told that for the first time the intercessory leaders were gathering together from all over Scotland. The next morning, as I came for breakfast, there was only one seat available, and it was right in the middle of those seasoned, godly intercessors.

As I sat down, I said: "Hi, I'm Dotty Schmitt from America, and I'm very eager to hear what God is saying to the intercessors in Scotland." The next two hours were absolutely memorable and faith inspiring. Our backgrounds and accents were very different, and even though we had never met one another, we were bonded together in the same family of God. Regardless of country, nationality, or language we are really one family in Jesus – how absolutely amazing!

When the members of the group were finally called into their specific meetings, I remained quietly sitting at the table pondering all we had discussed. I shared with my traveling companions that the fire, zeal, and passion for the Lord and for revival reflected and expressed in both the words and lives of these precious prayer leaders was life-changing for me. They were part of a thrust in Scotland called HOPE – Houses of Prayer Everywhere. Virtually all over Scotland, houses of prayer, praise and worship were being established. Special prayer and worship events were also being held in support of Israel. They were hearing that prayer and fasting were keys to the shaping of present history. Both here and in Ireland there was an emphasis of preparing the way of the Lord by equipping the Bride of Christ to stand in purity in these last days. While in Ireland we listened to some significant prophetic insights into the current happenings in Europe. In the United States we were hearing a similar cry, "Lord, give us the anointing that was upon the sons of Issachar."

> *. . .of the sons of Issachar who had*
> *understanding of the times,*
> *to know what Israel ought to do. . . .*
> I Chronicles 12:32

As we finished our time in those two beautiful countries, and began our flight into Israel, I heard Him ask, "What did you hear? What did you learn?" While I lay back on my seat I saw strong walls being built and upon them God was stationing the nations as warring intercessors. It was as if I could see a wall of fire being ignited from all over the earth as people increasingly gave a cry: "Maranatha, come, O Lord." Then the Scripture from Malachi 3:1 was illumined to me:

> *Behold, I send My messenger, and he will*
> *prepare the way before Me. And the Lord,*
> *whom you seek, will suddenly come to His*
> *temple, even the Messenger of the covenant, in*
> *whom you delight. Behold, He is coming, says*
> *the LORD of hosts.*
> Malachi 3:1

There is a cry from His church coming from all over the earth for Jesus to come! It's becoming clearer each day that He will first come *to* His Church in revival fire and then come *for* His Church. For those who have "ears to hear", the greatest harvest of souls ever will soon be gathered in!

As always our time in Israel was inspiring, exhausting, refreshing, and life-changing. Not only did I have the privilege of ministering to the beloved and stressed believers in the land, but we had the tremendous privilege of listening to and learning from seven different ministry leaders. To hear their biblical perspective on the land, the people, and the move of God increased my understanding of the times in which we live. I understood more clearly how Genesis 12:3 was a promise that was to chart the course of history:

> *I will bless those who bless you, and I will curse*
> *him who curses you; and in you all the families*
> *of the earth shall be blessed.*

To read Psalm 83:4 in the light of current events was very illuminating:

> *They have said, "Come, and let us cut them off*
> *from being a nation, that the name of Israel*
> *may be remembered no more."*

To further study the prophets through the eyes of the 21st century leads us to worship the Sovereign God of all the earth. The prophet Zechariah makes it quite clear that even in the midst of restoring the Jews to the land of Israel, Jerusalem (the city of peace) would increasingly become the city of turmoil, controversy, and upheaval. Israel would affect all the nations (one has only to observe the events at the United Nations as to its policies on Israel and the city of Jerusalem to better understand this).

> *Behold, I will make Jerusalem*
> *a cup of drunkenness to all the surrounding*
> *peoples, when they lay siege against Judah*
> *and Jerusalem.*
> Zechariah 12:2

When we compare Zechariah with Acts we understand better the reason for the intense conflict between light and darkness over the small piece of geography called Jerusalem.

> *And in that day His feet will stand on the*
> *Mount of Olives, which faces Jerusalem on the*
> *east. And the Mount of Olives shall be split in*
> *two, from east to west, making a very large*
> *valley; half of the mountain shall move toward*
> *the north and half of it toward the south.*
> Zechariah 14:4

> *"Men of Galilee, why do you stand gazing up*
> *into heaven? This same Jesus, who was taken*
> *up from you into heaven, will so come in like*
> *manner as you saw Him go into heaven."*
> Acts 1:11

The Mount of Olives from which Jesus ascended is the exact same place to which He shall descend in complete victory and triumph. Regardless of the present turmoil, He is Lord of Lords and King of Kings, and He will establish His kingdom forever and ever.

So much more was shared and discussed on the end-times and on the biblical perspectives of current and future events that a whole other book could be written (and many have and are), but let it presently suffice to state that I returned home a changed person. During the next months, I know that what I heard and received from the body of believers in these other nations infinitely changed the way I thought and how I daily lived my life!

One morning as I sat in the quiet of His Presence, I asked Him what it was that actually happened to me. "Lord, I feel more energized, more hungry for Your Presence, more intent on studying Your Scriptures and more desirous of bringing peace and kindness to all around me. What happened?" Suddenly I saw a big puzzle before me, and the various puzzle pieces were called biblical history, prophetic history, world history, and current events. I then saw the different pieces being put into place. A Scripture I had been reading came to me with great clarity:

In understanding there is a fountain of life. . .
Proverbs 16:22a NIV

"As you listened to My voice coming from the nations, especially in Israel, your understanding of My heart, ways, and purposes increased, and opened in you a deeper river of the fountain of life." As I pondered these words, I found myself smiling with delight. Indeed, rivers of joy and life were energizing my whole being.

Lord, may we increase in our listening capacities. Remove all dullness and distraction. In these critical days may we clearly hear what the Spirit is saying to the church today. Give us listening ears, and a tender heart to receive all You have for us in these strategic times."

WATCH AND PRAY

"Watch and pray, lest you enter into temptation. The spirit indeed is willing, but the flesh is weak."
Mark 14:38

*T*he Scriptures are like an exquisite diamond. As the light of God's Holy Spirit shines upon His Word, it too sparkles with fresh beauty and illumination that all the more captivates our hearts. Such was my recent experience in studying a very familiar passage. There are numerous different nuggets of truth locked into the profound account of Jesus' experience in the Garden of Gethsemane. I have feasted my soul on the extraordinary insights that this passage has revealed on both the humanity of Jesus, and the price He paid in His willingness to accomplish our redemption.

And He said, "Abba, Father,
all things are possible for You. Take this cup
away from Me; nevertheless, not what I will,
but what You will."
Mark 14:36

The loving tenderness expressed in the exchange between Father and Son is stunning to behold. How the Father's heart must have been moved as His Son cried out in anguish, "Abba, Daddy!"

It was a life-changing moment for me personally the day the Holy Spirit shone His light on this specific passage. The darkness and anguish of our present situation seemed at times to take my very breath away. As I cried out to Him in the dark confusion of my own broken heart, I saw His heart revealed in this passage. The Father's heart was also broken by what was happening in His Son's life. And I knew He also entered into the pain and brokenness of my own heart. Did our circumstances immediately change? No, but I had changed!

He had shown me more of Himself, and in beholding Him, I was changed. A trust and quiet peace began to fill my heart even in the turbulence of our situation.

Because this passage has such personal meaning for me, I have repeatedly studied it, and taught from it. Then recently, the Holy Spirit illumined another profound nugget of truth that I immediately knew would change the way I thought and prayed. The words "watch and pray" seemed to leap off the page. I heard His voice. "You are living in strategic times. And during these days, I am calling My people, not only into a deeper experience of prayer and intercession, but also into a greater revelation of what it means to be on 'watch' in these critical days."

As I studied the meaning of the word "watch," different words enhanced its meaning. To "watch" means to look, to see, to observe, to be awake, to be vigilant, to be alert.

And do this, knowing the time, that now it is
high time to awake out of sleep; for now our
salvation is nearer than when we first believed.
Romans 13:11

What exactly are we to watch, to observe? As I continued to study this theme of "watch and pray," I was amazed at how frequently the word "watch" is used in the Scripture, more than 300 times. It seems as if the Lord is always looking for watchmen, people who will carry His heart, His interests, His agenda; people who will see and observe what He sees, what He is watching. From this relationship of intimacy with the Father, we too, will watch with Him, and enter into the intercessions of His heart for our families, our congregations, our communities, our nation, and especially will we watch over world events and over Israel.

The Lord Himself is the chief Watchman, and it is from Him that we learn how to watch and pray.

He will not allow your foot to be moved; He
who keeps you will not slumber. Behold, He
who keeps Israel shall neither slumber nor
sleep. The Lord is your keeper; the Lord is
your shade at your right hand. The Lord shall
preserve you from all evil; He shall preserve
your soul. The Lord shall preserve your going

out and your coming in from this time forth,
and even forevermore.
Psalm 121:3-5,7,8

. . .Unless the Lord guards the city, the
watchman stays awake in vain.
Psalm 127:1b

Israel is especially strategic in the unfolding of end-time events, and increasingly God is calling people from all over the earth to "watch and pray" for His covenant nation.

I have set watchmen on your walls, O
Jerusalem; they shall never hold their peace
day or night. You who make mention of the
Lord, do not keep silent, and give Him no rest
till He establishes and till He makes Jerusalem a
praise in the earth.
Isaiah 62:6,7

A careful study of Luke 21 and Matthew 24 yields much treasure of understanding to those who are lovers of truth. In the midst of answering the probing prophetic questions of His disciples concerning end-time events Jesus tells us what to watch for:

Now as He sat on the Mount of Olives, the
disciples came to Him privately, saying, "Tell
us, when will these things be? And what will be
the sign of Your coming, and of the end of the
age?" And Jesus answered and said to them:
"Watch out that no one deceives you."
Matthew 24:3,4 NIV

Deception and end-time events seem to run concurrently. To be in an obedient, loving relationship with the Lord Jesus and with His people is expedient in these last days. To immerse ourselves in the person and work of Jesus, to be lovers and students of Truth, flows out of our commitment to watch and pray with the Lover of our souls.

Recently, my attention was arrested by Jesus' words in Luke 21:34,35:

"But take heed to yourselves,
lest your hearts be weighed down with
carousing, drunkenness, and cares of this life,
and that Day come on you unexpectedly. For it
will come as a snare on all those who dwell on
the face of the whole earth."

It is obvious that we are called to personally watch for those things that cause us to become easily distracted, anxious, and dull to the voice of the Lord and to the signs of the times. An alternative translation for the Word escape is "to pass safely through." I am convinced that Daniel was one who knew how to watch and pray, and as a result he was able to safely pass through every evil plot of the enemy, and to stand at the end of his life as an elder, a prophetic statesman of intercession, bringing complete delight to the courts of heaven.

And he said to me, "O Daniel, man greatly
beloved, understand the words that I speak to
you, and stand upright, for I have now been

*sent to you." While he was speaking this word
to me, I stood trembling.*
Daniel 10:11

Of the many things the Lord is diligently watching, and over which He is calling us to watch and pray with Him, two are most strategic in preparing for His soon return. The account of Matthew 23 is a beautiful insight into Jesus' heart as it pertains to His ancient people Israel.

*"O Jerusalem, Jerusalem, the one who kills the
prophets and stones those who are sent to her!
How often I wanted to gather your children
together, as a hen gathers her chicks under
her wings, but you were not willing! See! Your
house is left to you desolate; for I say to you,
you shall see Me no more till you say, 'Blessed
is He who comes in the name of the Lord!'"*
Matthew 23:37-39

Luke tells us Jesus wept over the rejection of His people, but there is also an extraordinary glimmer of hope locked into this lament. There is a clear implication that His return is vitally linked to His people acknowledging and welcoming Him. In all prior centuries the power of these Scriptures has been somewhat obscured, but in 1967 something strategic happened both in Israel and in the church. For the first time in 2,000 years, Israel recaptured Jerusalem as its capital, and the Holy Spirit was being poured out upon a very lost, yet seeking, generation of young people. The "Jesus People" movement swept across this nation, and amongst those Jesus apprehended were hundreds and hundreds of natural-born

Jews. Charles and I will forever be grateful for the privilege of getting to know and disciple many of these young Messianic believers, especially up at Camp Dominion in Northern Minnesota. Many of these young hippies, some thirty years later, are now living in Israel and raising up a cry of welcome to Yeshua from all over the land. "Blessed is He who comes in the name of the Lord."

Another strategic arena where Jesus is calling us to watch and pray with Him is in regard to the nations.

> *"And this gospel of the kingdom will be*
> *preached in all the world as a witness to all the*
> *nations, and then the end will come."*
> Matthew 24:14

The thrust of the church into world missions, from every nation, is unprecedented. There is a deep awakening happening both in the church and in the Messianic community of believers in Israel to preach the Gospel in all the earth. The Lord strategically linked His second coming to both Israel welcoming Him, and the Gospel being preached in all the earth. If ever there were an hour for us to be diligent, alert, and watchful, it is now! Listen to Jesus' imploring command and clear directive to us:

> *"Watch therefore, for you do not know what*
> *hour your Lord is coming. But know this, that if*
> *the master of the house had known what hour*
> *the thief would come, he would have watched*
> *and not allowed his house to be broken into.*

Therefore you also be ready, for the Son of Man
is coming at an hour you do not expect."
Matthew 24:42-44

These present days and those before us will produce much fear and anxiety in those who are lulled to sleep. However, it will be much different for those who are wide awake and "watching and praying" with the chief Watchman. As I was pondering these most sobering passages and dire future events, I found myself sighing before the Lord. "Lord, what will be the secret of these last days for Your people? How will we not only endure, but how will we be prophetic watchmen and intercessors, and not fall asleep on You, as Your early disciples did?" I felt His smile wash over my spirit, and in an instant I knew:

"Do not grieve, for the joy of the LORD
is your strength."
Nehemiah 8:10c NIV

"These things I have spoken to you,
that My joy may remain in you,
and that your joy may be full."
John 15:11

God is positioning His worshipping watchmen all over the world, but in the midst of intense watching and praying, He is also giving us the gift of laughter and celebration because we have indeed seen the end of the matter.

. . .looking unto Jesus, the author and finisher
of our faith, who for the joy that was set before

Him endured the cross, despising the shame,
and has sat down at the right hand of the
throne of God.
Hebrews 12:2

Just as our beloved, prophetic High Priest of intercession endured the cross because of the joy of victory and triumph set before Him, so too will we be praying watchman
who enter into His joy and laughter during these days.

And the ransomed of the Lord shall return,
and come to Zion with singing, with everlasting
joy on their heads. They shall obtain joy
and gladness, and sorrow and sighing
shall flee away.
Isaiah 35:10

Thank You, Lord, for Your invitation to "watch and pray"
with You in this pivotal prophetic season of history. By
Your grace we will worship and watch with You.

ON WHOSE SHOULDERS DO YOU STAND?

And the things that you have heard
from me among many witnesses,
commit these to faithful men who will
be able to teach others also.
II Timothy 2:2

*T*his small verse describes a vast sphere of influence. It contains four levels of mentoring and discipling – Paul imparting to Timothy, Timothy imparting to reliable men, and these men in turn imparting to others. As I was studying the subject of impartation, mentoring, and discipling, I heard the Lord probing my own heart: "And on whose shoulders do you stand My daughter? Who imparted to you? Who are your teachers and mentors? Who are those who have most influenced your life in your walk with Me?" I quickly made note of each of these questions, and then began to reflect back with deep gratitude to the many godly men and women who have poured into my own life, not only through their teachings, but also through their Presence, example, and lifestyle.

While I was prayerfully considering who most influenced me, I began to explore why their lives so marked and impacted mine. In this process of explorating what discipling and influencing others really involved, I came across a quote by Dr. A. W. Tozer (1897-1963). After spending many years immersing himself in the great Christian teachers and theologians of both past and present, Dr. Tozer penned this challenging statement: "Come near to the holy men and women of the past and you will soon feel the heat of their desire after God. They mourned for Him, they prayed and wrestled and sought for Him, day and night, in season and out, and when they had found Him the finding was all the sweeter for the long seeking."

As I reflected on that inspiring quote, I thought back to the time when I first heard Dr. Tozer preach. It was in 1961 at the Gospel Tabernacle on 8th Avenue and 42nd Street in New York City. (It is noteworthy to mention that I was with a group of young adults who were so hungry for the Lord that we would travel all over New York City by subway and bus just to learn and receive from those who had walked with Him for many years.) What was it about this old, frail man of God that even to this day I can recall his teaching, illustrations, and the hunger he stirred within me for the Lord? I remember Dr. Tozer walking back and forth on the platform as he unfolded the story of Enoch, the man who walked with God. The Presence of God was richly on him as he said, "And one day, as God and Enoch enjoyed walking together, the Lord stopped and turned to Enoch and said, 'Enoch, we're so much closer to My home than to yours, why don't you just come all the way home with Me today?'" I still remember thinking, O, Lord, I want to have that kind of relationship with You! How true is the verse from Proverbs 13:14 (NASB), which says:

The teaching of the wise is a fountain of life. . . .

Recently, as Charles and I were enjoying a time of relaxation and vacation, we also had a concentrated opportunity to simply study, write, and reflect on the goodness and faithfulness of the Lord. During dinner one evening, I asked Charles who he considered to be the key mentors and teachers in his life. For the next two hours, we sat at the dinner table sharing our hearts. We wept and laughed at all the memories of those who helped us, corrected us, inspired us, taught us, and challenged us. We even found ourselves thankful for those with whom we had great conflict and turmoil. We talked about those who, especially in our younger years, tried to bring correction and adjustment to us, and how, in our own insecurities and arrogance, we often resisted and fought, and sadly, eventually separated from. Through all of these experiences and interactions, essential lessons and truths were being poured into us. Our conclusion was that we had personally experienced the following promise of the Lord at work in our lives again and again!

And we know that all things work together for
good to those who love God, to those who are
the called according to His purpose.
Romans 8:28

The defining words in this passage are "those who love Him." In our journey with the Lord, through all the successes and failures, the most critical issue was and is, do we love Him? When we deeply love Him, no matter how often we stumble, we will get up again because His loving-kindness is better than life itself.

> *Do not rejoice over me, my enemy; when I fall,*
> *I will arise; when I sit in darkness, the Lord will*
> *be a light to me.*
> Micah 7:8

Jesus taught us much about mentoring and discipling. He could always see and call forth the potential of His disciples when, as yet, they were still fickle and immature followers. He cultivated a life-changing friendship with them. Through many, challenging conflicts and crises, they eventually became His intimate friends upon whom He could depend to change the world with His Gospel of salvation and peace.

As Charles and I continued to discuss who our mentors were, we realized that we had known many levels of impartation and relationship. To cultivate an attitude of wanting to learn from every relationship and every experience has certainly enriched us. First of all, we have learned much from deeply studying the Scriptures. Above all, study, meditation, and obedience to the Word of God has most molded and formed us. We both concluded that we owed the most to those who taught us how to study the Scriptures for ourselves. As teenagers, we belonged to a high-school organization called Hi. B.A. (High-school Born Againers). We met weekly after school to discuss what we learned from our daily quiet time in the Scriptures. Little did we realize then that we were learning invaluable lessons on digging into the Word of God for ourselves. Then in college I became part of a vibrant college ministry called Inter-Varsity Christian Fellowship. The quality of life demonstrated by the staff, the warm and encouraging peer friendship, and the weekly inductive Bible study discussions were life-changing for me. Learning to study the Bible inductively became a life-long discipline. In its simplest form, the inductive study method asks three questions – what does this passage say, what does it mean, and how does this passage apply to me personally? Using these simple questions, our college group discovered priceless treasure, especially in the books of *John* and *Romans*. The proverbial statement that it is better to teach someone how to fish rather than to fish for them is certainly most applicable in the study of the Scriptures.

Through the study of Scripture, our growing knowledge of church history, and the diligent reading of the biographies of great men and women of God, both from the past and present, an indelible mark was made upon our lives. We learned much about the Christian life from these resources. Especially in our younger years, we realized how deeply influenced we were by Christian leaders and teachers. As we discussed both our positive and negative experiences, James 3:1 became even more meaningful to us, for it is a serious, as well as a blessed admonition to those who to teach the Scriptures:

> *My brethren, let not many of you become*
> *teachers, knowing that we shall receive a*
> *stricter judgment.*

Nurturing healthy, transparent peer relationships was a key ingredient to our maturing in the Lord. Cultivating a culture of humility and honor towards others always opens up for us greater treasure in our knowledge of the Lord Jesus.

As Charles and I concluded our very meaningful and inspiring discussion on those from whom we have learned and received, we looked at one another and both verbalized the same challenging question. Who will stand upon our shoulders? Will our "ceiling" become the "floor" for the next generation of believers? Will the truth and biblical revelation that have become essential foundations in our lives be imparted to those who follow us? Does our Presence and lifestyle inspire others to love Him more?

Are we effectively preparing another generation who are radical in their obedience to the Lord, passionate in their love for Him, and intense in the love of His Truth and of His Presence? As Charles and I joined hands across the dinner table, this became our cry and prayer to Him for the next generation. Even as we have repeatedly experienced fresh revival moves of His Spirit, so we pray that the Lord will once again powerfully pour out His Spirit upon all of us in this present generation!

"And it shall come to pass in the last days, says God, that I will pour out of My Spirit on all flesh; your sons and your daughters shall prophesy, your young men shall see visions, your old men shall dream dreams. And on My menservants and on My maidservants I will

On Whose Shoulders Do You Stand?

pour out My Spirit in those days;
and they shall prophesy."
Acts 2:17,18

May you who have journeyed with me through these pages, come to your own personal joy of discovery! Jesus alone, is worthy of all of our love and adoration, obedience, and service! May you consistently be speechless with wonder and joy at the unfolding treasure you discover in our magnificent God and Savior and may you become exceedingly "rich toward God."

Father, Thank You for Your amazing grace and lavish love. May we, Your people, live in such a way that those who follow us can stand on our shoulders and go further than we have ever gone in fulfilling Your plans and purposes for their lives and for their generation.

Now to Him who is able to do exceedingly
abundantly above all that we ask or think,
according to the power that works in us, to
Him be glory in the church by Christ Jesus to all
generations, forever and ever. Amen.
Ephesians 3:20-21